D0061331

The Child as Critic

*Teaching Literature
in Elementary and Middle Schools*

DISCARD
Otterbein University
CourtrightMemorialLib
Otterbein College
Westerville, Ohio 43081

NEW AIMS IN CHILDREN'S LITERATURE

Leland B. Jacobs, General Editor

Second Edition

The Child as Critic

Teaching Literature
in Elementary and Middle Schools

GLENNA DAVIS SLOAN

TEACHERS COLLEGE, COLUMBIA UNIVERSITY
NEW YORK AND LONDON

Published by Teachers College Press, 1234 Amsterdam Avenue, New York, N.Y. 10027

Copyright © 1984 by Teachers College, Columbia University

All rights reserved. No part of this publication may be reproduced or transmitted in any form or by any means, electronic or mechanical, including photocopy, or any information storage and retrieval system, without permission from the publisher.

The original edition of this work appeared under the title *The Child as Critic: Teaching Literature in the Elementary School*. Copyright © 1975 by Teachers College, Columbia University

Library of Congress Cataloging in Publication Data

Sloan, Glenna Davis, 1930–
    The child as critic.

    Bibliography: p.
    Includes index.
    1. Literature—Study and teaching (Elementary) 2. Language arts (Elementary) I. Title.
LB1575.S53   1984   372.6′4   84-2767

ISBN 0-8077-2705-9

Manufactured in the United States of America

89   88   87   3   4   5   6

(Copyright page continued on page xiv.)

To Jake, Charles and Mark

Contents

Foreword

This book seeks to explain what the real place of literature is in primary education. Its place is to provide the verbal element in the training of the imagination. The imagination is not a self-indulgent, ornamental, or escapist faculty: it is the constructive power of the mind. Hence one should teach reading neither efficiently nor passively: reading has to be a continuously active and leisurely growth, as all genuine growth is. Because it is active, the teaching of writing is inseparably a part of the teaching of reading, and the aim of teaching a child to write poetry is not to produce poets, but to produce articulate people, articulateness being the highest form of freedom that society can give to the individual. Mrs. Sloan quotes Kenneth Koch, who should know, as remarking that teaching children to write in this way is not really "teaching," in the limited sense, so much as a matter of allowing them to discover and exploit what they already have.

The author makes clear from the beginning her opposition to what she calls the "skills and drills" approach, which frustrates and stunts all genuine imaginative growth. Emphasis on skills tries to be efficient: it regards learning to read as a largely mechanical operation, to be taught with the least waste of time by repetition of familiar words, adding new words gradually as facility is gained. The argument for such teaching seems extremely plausible, and has only the flaw that the human mind, which always begins as a child's mind, is simply not built that way. Consequently such an approach is not merely immoral and anti-intellectual, it is also miserably inefficient, even in its own terms. Emphasis on drills is, again, an emphasis on a "teaching" process in which the teacher is the active agent, the one who knows, and the students are passive, learning through a mechanism of imitation. That doesn't work either.

I have had no firsthand experience with education below the university level, and while I believe that no theory of criticism is any good at all unless it can be adapted to kindergarten and grade one, I naturally make mistakes when I try to suggest how such an adaptation could proceed. I think most of my mistakes have really been much the same mistake: the mistake of underestimating what a child can respond to. Mrs. Sloan, with more experience, does not make this mistake. She knows that children can respond to tragedy and irony as well as to comedy and romance, and that children want difficulty: if they are practicing jumping over hurdles, they want the highest hurdle they can possibly get over, not a low one that they know they can manage. The author also makes it clear that the notion of there being some danger of distorting "reality" by introducing fantasy and myth to the small child is pure (except that it is very impure) superstition. Such dangers only arise in certain types of bad realism. As C. S. Lewis remarks, no child is going to confuse *Alice in Wonderland* with reality, but a pseudo-realistic story about life in a British public school might lead him to expect that school life really was like this. Mrs. Sloan notes that there is now a fashion for realism in children's stories, probably because there is also a fashion for fantasy in adult stories, and adults tend to expect children to make up for their own deficiencies.

When I was about ten I once had to mind the little boy next door, who was about three. He wanted to know what the flowers in the front yard were. I told him they were hydrangeas, and this word, which came out something like "hyainzuz," he repeated all afternoon, chuckling to himself at intervals. Many years later I realized that I had confronted that afternoon one of the primary phenomena of literary education. It is the rare magic word, the mysterious polysyllabic word, that is most likely to become the educational focus, the beckoning light ahead: similarly, it is the magic story, not the imaginatively squalid story, that is most likely to start the quest for awareness going. Ultimately, everyone exposed to literary education has to try to become a Prospero, otherwise he becomes a Caliban. From the stuttering Dick-and-Jane readers to the foul-mouthed blither of the Watergate transcripts, we realize how many Calibans there are who are quite right in saying:

> You taught me language; and my profit on't
> Is, I know how to curse.

But there are still some Prosperos who have learned how to control the magic of words and make it part of their own experience, and it is to increase their number in society that the present book is devoted.

NORTHROP FRYE

Acknowledgments

(This is a continuation of the copyright page.)

Grateful acknowledgment is made for permission to reprint the following selections:

"Swing Song" from *The Little Hill* by Harry Behn. Copyright 1949 by Harry Behn; renewed 1977 by Alice L. Behn. Reprinted by permission of Harcourt Brace Jovanovich, Inc.

"When my canary" from *Cricket Songs: Japanese Haiku*. Translated by Harry Behn, copyright © 1964 by Harry Behn. Reprinted by permission of Harcourt Brace Jovanovich, Inc., and Curtis Brown, Ltd.

"Dark Girl" from *Personals* by Arna Bontemps. Copyright 1963 by Arna Bontemps. Reprinted by permission of Harold Ober Associates, Inc.

"A City Park" from *A Family Album and Other Poems* by Alter Brody. Copyright 1918 by B. W. Huebsch, Inc. and renewed 1946 by Alter Brody. Reprinted by permission of Viking Penguin Inc.

"Wild Geese" by Elinor Chipp. Reprinted by permission of Branden Press, Inc.

"I Am" by Hilda Conkling. Copyright 1920 and renewed 1948 by Hilda Conkling. Reprinted by permission of Random House, Inc.

"The Goblin" from *Picture Rhymes from Foreign Lands* by Rose Fyleman (J. B. Lippincott Co.). Copyright 1935 and renewed 1963 by Rose Fyleman. Reprinted by permission of Harper & Row, Publishers, Inc., and The Society of Authors as the literary representative of the Estate of Rose Fyleman.

"Transcontinent" by Donald Hall. Reprinted by permission of the author.

"In Time of Silver Rain" from *Selected Poems of Langston Hughes*. Copyright 1938 and renewed 1966 by Langston Hughes. Reprinted by permission of Alfred A. Knopf, Inc.

"Stars" and "Heaven" from *Selected Poems of Langston Hughes*. Copyright 1947 by Langston Hughes. Reprinted by permission of Alfred A. Knopf, Inc.

"City Autumn" from *On City Streets* by Joseph Moncure March published by M. Evans and Company, Inc., and Bantam Books, Inc.

"The Pickety Fence" from *One at a Time* by David McCord. Copyright 1952 by David McCord. First appeared in *Far and Few* by David McCord. Reprinted by permission of Little, Brown and Company. Also appeared in *Every Time I Climb a Tree*. Reprinted by permission of Curtis Brown, Ltd. Copyright 1925, 1929, 1949, 1950, 1952 by David McCord.

Excerpt from "What Is White" from *Hailstones and Halibut Bones* by Mary LeDuc O'Neill. Copyright 1961 by Mary LeDuc O'Neill. Reprinted by permission of Doubleday and Company, Inc., and World's Work, Ltd.

"Things to Remember" from *The Blackbird in the Lilac* by James Reeves. Copyright 1952 by James Reeves. Reprinted by permission of the author and Oxford University Press, London.

"The People" and "The Firefly" from *Under the Tree* by Elizabeth Madox Roberts. Copyright 1922 by B. W. Huebsch, Inc. Copyright renewed 1950 by Ivor S. Roberts. Copyright 1930 by the Viking Press, Inc. Copyright renewed 1958 by Ivor S. Roberts and Viking Penguin Inc. Reprinted by permission of Viking Penguin Inc.

"The Toaster" from *Laughing Time: Nonsense Poems* by William Jay Smith, published by Delacorte Press, 1980. Copyright © 1955, 1957, 1980 by William Jay Smith. Reprinted by permission of William Jay Smith and Delacorte Press/Seymour Lawrence.

"Up in the Air" from *I Go A-Traveling* by James S. Tippett. Copyright 1929 by Harper & Row, Publishers, Inc. Copyright renewed 1957 by James S. Tippett. Reprinted by permission of Harper & Row, Publishers, Inc.

"Roads Go Ever Ever On" by J. R. R. Tolkien from *The Hobbit*. Reprinted by permission of Houghton Mifflin Company.

"December" by Sanderson Vanderbilt from *Creative Youth* by Hughes Mearns. Copyright 1925 by Doubleday and Company, Inc. Reprinted by permission of the publisher.

"Child Lonely Playing," "If I Could Fly," "A Beautiful Bird," "The Darkening Clouds," "Hovering over us" from *Poetic Composition Through the Grades* by Robert A. Wolsch, pages 153, 87, 68, 104. Copyright 1970 by Robert A. Wolsch. Reprinted by permission of Teachers College Press.

Excerpt from *Sounds of a Distant Drum*, Teacher's Edition, by Bill Martin, Jr. Copyright 1967 by Holt, Rinehart & Winston. Used by permission of the publisher.

Lines from *Millions of Cats* by Wanda Gag. Copyright 1928 by Coward-McCann, Inc., copyright renewed © 1956 by Robert Janssen. Reprinted by permission of Coward-McCann, Inc.

General Editor's Introduction

Throughout the history of elementary education in North America, literature has had a place in children's schooling. To be sure, the reasons for the inclusion of literature in the curriculum and the emphases in teaching with it have differed from era to era. But the belief that literature is of importance in children's schooling persists.

In the past, literature has frequently been exploited to patriotic, character-development, or moralistic ends as well as being used as motivation for other kinds of content. On these pages, however, Glenna Davis Sloan goes well beyond many of the traditional proposals for literature in the elementary and the middle school, since she views literature as a significant inclusion in the curriculum for its own sake and on its own terms. She recognizes that, as thought about aesthetic feeling, story and poem are more than isolated, unrelated excursions into what is delightful. She views children's literary experiences as cumulative and encompassing. Too, she makes clear that one cannot "teach" literature. One can make the literature available to girls and boys by reading to them, reading with them, and making it possible for them to read on their own. As soon as the child has the story or poem in mind, the literature is possessed. Therefore, what can be taught follows, and that is criticism, to the end of developing in the child an "educated imagination."

In order to help children become critics, through appropriate classroom practices, there must be a theoretical base in which such practices find their bearings. For such theoretical bearings Dr. Sloan accepts Northrop Frye's beliefs about what literature is and how it serves human kind. She interprets Frye's structural principles and his proposals for the criticism of literature, as they can be applied to a literature program for the young. From Dr. Sloan's consideration of what literature is and what it does for the individual, she concludes that it is at the center of a child's education and is "the most effective 'reading program' ever devised."

From her background of having been a successful classroom teacher, Dr. Sloan knows well that what ultimately affects children's responses to literature are the practices that the teacher uses to guide the child in enjoying a story or poem. Therefore she presents a variety of teaching procedures and classroom activities that foster children's abilities as critics. She clearly shows how theory and practice serve children as they develop educated imaginations. And since "literature begets literature," Dr. Sloan's consideration of children's original composing as an integral part of literary criticism is directly on target.

While it is true that the school is responsible for children becoming skillful readers, that is only the beginning. To become a critical reader of both informational writing and prose fiction and poetry is why one becomes skillful. And it is as important to be a critical reader of literature as it is to be a critical reader of what is factual. It is to the child becoming a critical reader of imaginative literature that Dr. Sloan gives attention and thus makes a much-needed contribution on the following pages.

LELAND B. JACOBS

Introduction

So often, at every level from grade school to college, the study of literature is fragmented. We read this poem, that play, these novels, and examine each as a separate entity. While the study of each separate work is a valid and important aspect of literary criticism, the examination too frequently ends only in cruel vivisection of a work or endless commentary on some aspects of its content. Both as a student and as a teacher I found this fragmentation and subsequent dilution of the power of literature disappointing and unsatisfying. If students are to experience the full impact of literature, they have to encounter it as a cumulative study that adds up to more than a list of apparently unconnected poems and stories. For this to be possible, literary study has to be set within the framework of a theory of literature.

Northrop Frye, the eminent literary critic, has provided such a theory with his delineation of the structural principles of literature and his formulation furnishes the basis for the literary study described in this book. The practice set forth here shows that the study of literature is indeed a cumulative one and that significant beginnings may be made in it in the elementary school, with materials and methods appropriate for use with young children.

The Child as Critic is intended for teachers, prospective teachers, language arts supervisors, designers of curriculum, and others interested in the teaching of English in elementary and middle schools. It combines theory and practice in the belief that effective practice can only be developed where there is a theoretical understructure of consequence. This book proposes a way of unifying the language arts in a program that makes literature the center of

language studies. In this proposal literary study is broadly conceived to include both the experiencing of literature and a variety of
responses to it, verbal and nonverbal. The primary aim of the
program is to foster genuine literacy, something that develops out of
a love for language and an awareness of its infinite possibilities,
both outgrowths of an abundance of pleasurable experiences with
fine literature.

Why is it important that young children study literature? What
is involved in the study? How exactly do you "teach" literature?
What can be done in the elementary school to prepare children for
advanced literary studies? These are some of the questions that *The
Child as Critic* endeavors to answer.

There are many valid reasons why literature should be part of a
child's education; Chapter 1 reviews three of the most important.
Chapter 2 is concerned with a definition central to the book: what it
means to "teach" and "study" literature. Chapters 3 and 4 provide
the foundation of literary theory necessary for the development of
learning sequences that will lead to significant literary understandings. Educational and literary theory are translated into practice in
Chapters 5 through 7, where numerous examples of teaching strategies may be found. These include specifics related to planning
lessons designed to foster literary understandings; details as to
procedures, such as discussion techniques; and suggestions for suitable content to use in learning sequences.

The other side of the coin, composition, is considered here as an
integral part of the study of literature, and Chapter 8 details
procedures useful in helping children compose stories and poems of
their own. Included in the book is an annotated list of selected
professional references as well as a bibliography of all the poems
and stories cited. In the case of traditional tales, care was taken to
list an outstanding retelling or edition. Students of children's literature will find this bibliography a comprehensive selection of readings in the field.

The revised edition of *The Child as Critic* contains the same
material as the first edition together with a number of additions and
amplifications. Chapter 1 now includes a discussion of the central
role that literature plays in the development of literacy. In Chapter
2 there is a new section, entitled "How Children Develop as Critics,"
that details stages in the development of literary understandings.
Chapter 5, "Theory into Practice," is enlarged to include, along with
an overview of the literary theory described in this book, practical
suggestions for implementing it in practice. This chapter now in-

cludes an extensive bibliography of stories and poems suitable for reading aloud, as well as specific suggestions for planning classroom programs in independent (individualized) reading. The section "Asking Literary Questions" in Chapter 7 has been expanded, and many additional specific strategies for teaching the literary criticism described in the theoretical sections of the book are now part of this chapter. Throughout the revised edition many more titles of children's books are included as examples and illustrations.

GLENNA DAVIS SLOAN

The Child as Critic

*Teaching Literature
in Elementary and Middle Schools*

Chapter 1

The Case for Literature

Literacy is everyone's concern: educators, parents, employers, and perhaps most of all, the young people who reach high school age with fourth-grade reading skills. In recent years we have seen a proliferation of methods for teaching children to decode printed symbols, the first step in the complex process of becoming an effective, independent reader. The literate person, however, is not one who knows *how* to read, but *one who reads*: fluently, responsively, critically, and because he wants to. Reading involves an engagement with print and an active personal involvement with the ideas expressed in it.

Children will become readers only if their emotions have been engaged, their imaginations stirred and stretched by what they find on printed pages. One way—a sure way—to make this happen is through literature, imaginative literature in particular, where ideally language is used with intensity and power in a direct appeal to the feelings and the imagination. This literature, writing that has claim to consideration on the basis of its beauty of form and its emotional power, is the most effective "reading program" ever devised.

There are those who shunt literature aside with the argument that elementary education must above all be practical. And since literature addresses itself to the imagination, many teachers can accept it only as a diversion or recreation. It must make way for the more serious business of addressing the reason through down-to-earth instruction in reading. Confronted with low reading-test scores and children who read "below grade level" or not at all, many elementary educators insist that their only legitimate business is the teaching of reading "skills." Too often this means the implementation of a tedious remediation program designed to drill into the child the dullest mechanics of the reading process. For someone who has already learned to hate reading there could hardly be a more futile approach. Drills of skills will not generate interest in reading if none has ever been aroused. Literature nourishes the imagination and develops the desire to read. Children will always be more absorbed in the exploits of Horton the Elephant and Curious George than in the vagaries of long and short vowel sounds.

This is not to say that basic skills need not be taught and developed. But they will be more readily learned and used only if the child, from the earliest age, is continuously made aware that reading is worth his time and attention. Participation in a reading program that does not go beyond drills of skills is like learning to play the piano by practicing scales without ever playing a piece of music.

Nothing is more important or practical in the long run than literature. Nothing should come before it. All efforts to teach reading must begin with it. Literature appeals directly to the emotions and the imagination, carrying within a powerful motivation to participate in its wonders and delights. It is only the *art* of literature that can successfully counter the drawing power of television and mass media.

The slowest learner will profit less from extra doses of dull drill than he will from the injections for the imagination that literature can provide. Furthermore, the ability of the child to experience a story or poem is not dependent upon his ability to decode or read fluently. He, like the telegraph operator, is able to "read" what he hears. Although being read to is not reading for oneself, it is unquestionably the prerequisite for developing a desire to do so.

The Primacy of Poetry

We are constantly told that if we expect instruction to be successful we must begin where the child is. *Imaginative literature is exactly where he is.* Not only are his interests and emotions aroused by it, but it is also closer to his natural mode of expression than other, more utilitarian, uses of language. The imaginative writer, particularly the poet, constantly makes use of analogy and identity, simile and metaphor. So does the child. His thinking and the language that reveals it is characteristically an implied simile: something is like something else in some way.

It is natural for children to make free use of metaphor. A child with a stomach-ache complains that his stomach is "broken." Another looks in awe at his grandmother's varicose veins and asks why her legs are "all thunder and lightning."

In *The Lore and Language of School Children*, Iona and Peter Opie show how children's names for things often come close to poetic expression, at least in the sense of being metaphorical. A boy's mouth is his "cake-hole," his stomach is his "breadbasket," large feet are "beetle crushers." As indicated through their lore and language, children delight in nonsense rhymes, rhythmic chants, riddles, codes, epithets, and all forms of word play or metaphorical use of language. Like the primitive poets they resemble, children delight in unlocking the word-hoard with lists of strange names, jingles that teach the alphabet, and rhymes that offer keys to history: "Columbus sailed the ocean blue, / In fourteen hundred and ninety-two."

Children's oral lore shows that they are explorers and lovers of language, just as the poet is. They love to pun, to play with words, to ask riddles in which words with similar sounds are bandied: "What did the ear hear? Only the nose knows." They can make nouns do the work of verbs in riddles, if not on standardized tests: "Why did the window box? Because it saw the garden fence." Like poets, children are fascinated by all the marvelous things that words can do.

The language of poetry is rhythmic and repetitive; so is the natural expression of the child. Movement and language are inextricably bound together in children. They are kinesthetic creatures who delight in moving to rhythmic chants made of words that take their fancy. Their natural speech is repetitive, heavily accented, and prolix; given to sing-song, whine, chant, and crooning.

Poetry is a method of thought as well as a means of expression. In many ways it is a primitive method of thought with a logic of its own that has nothing to do with verifiable proofs. The poet has license to say that two quite unlike things are like each other, even that they *are* each other. The prose of the highly advanced technological society with its jargon and high level of abstraction bears little relationship to poetry. We tend to think, since we are surrounded by it, that this prose is the natural way to speak and write. But if prose is more natural than poetry, how is it that the simplest societies create poetry, whereas prose is always a much later and specialized development of civilization?

Long before a society has prose it has poetry, understood as a method of thought as well as a means of expression. As every reader of myth and legend knows, primitive poetry delights in catalogues:

long lists of strange names, names that are potent in magic, that are keys to history, that summon up the deeds of heroes and gods. In this poetry everyday language is conventionalized, ordered to form, shaped, and controlled.

In simpler societies poetry emerges as a primary need because it is seen as a simple and direct means of expression. In Eskimo, for instance, the word *anerca* means "poetry"; it also means "to breathe." Primitive poetry is linked to movement, to the basic bodily rhythms involved in singing, dancing, and marching. Children, if they are freed to do so, recapitulate the experience of primitive literature. They turn far more easily to the rhythmic, the conventionalized, to riddles, conundrums, and stylized jingles than to the abstract prose of the classroom text. Riddles, where things are described in terms of other things—the very essence of poetic thought—are a special delight.

What child would not be intrigued in figuring out this riddle of a needle and thread?

> Old Mother Twitchett has but one eye,
> And a long tail which she can let fly;
> And every time she goes over a gap,
> She leaves a bit of her tail in a trap.

Such poetry and the way of looking at the world that it embodies makes a direct appeal to a child's intellectual excitement. He wants to "guess" and more often than not he guesses quickly and correctly. The mental processes involved in making riddles, proceeding through pun and identification, are very close to a child's own.

We complain that education inhibits spontaneity of expression; it is more likely that a prosaic literary education is the inhibitor. How many times have we found that children treat classroom prose as though it were a dead language, something they try to read and write that bears no relation to the way they speak?

In an attempt to be practical and utilitarian, we ignore the child's natural development. His literary education begins with prose, a prose that is to him nothing more than a foreign language found only in textbooks. Imaginative literature, in particular poetry, is set aside as an extra, to be used as a supplement to the practical program of learning to read and write no-nonsense prose. But poetry *is* a legitimate mode of thought, as legitimate as prose and far more basic.

Figurative language, the staple of poetry and all imaginative literature, is not an embellishment. Figures of speech are not ornaments of thought, not verbal gargoyles, but direct expressions of strong feeling. Without their use our language becomes too abstract and mechanical. Poetry's use of metaphor and visualized imagery makes it a most concrete means of expression. It subordinates logic and sequence to the insights of simile and metaphor.

From rhythmic verse we get a sense of energy and timing, a sense of language disciplined yet filled with a life that evokes a bodily response. An early and pleasurable immersion in poetry—nursery rhymes, jingles, counting songs, rhythmic and imagistic verse of all kinds—is the best introduction to reading and at the same time a defense against literary banality of all kinds. It is also a prerequisite for learning to write.

Good writing has to be based on good speech and good speech is a logical though complex development from natural speech. If we write in a way we never speak our writing is certain to lack conviction and personality. A child's unpunctuated outpourings are neither prose nor poetry but they are *closer* to poetry than to prose. The child, like the primitive poet, seems to understand that verse rather than prose is a simpler and more direct way to conventionalize natural speech. Outside the classroom, at least, the child's speech is filled with chanting and singing as well as such primitive verse forms as the war-cry and the taunt-song.

Through a series of unusually fine literary "readers," Holt, Rinehart & Winston's Sounds of Language, educator Bill Martin, Jr., shows how children's own jingles and rhymes can be used effectively in an instructional program to develop literacy. Familiar rhythmic chants like "Happy Birthday to You" and lyrics from songs children know by ear are included, along with fine prose writing, in this unique set of texts designed for use throughout elementary and middle school grades. In Sounds of Language the child's natural propensity for rhythmic language and word play is capitalized on. The predictability of language patterns is a built-in aid in learning to read; in rhymed verse this predictability is pleasurably emphasized. Verse and chant naturally employ the repetition of words and phrases that is artifically and often awkwardly developed for reading material in conventional basal readers (sequential series of books designed to teach reading through the systematic introduction of controlled vocabulary). Suggestions for teachers that accompany the Sounds series emphasize the importance of *hearing* language to the process of learning to read it.

Consider the young child
who has frequently heard his teacher read

> One misty, moisty morning
> When cloudy was the weather,
>   I chanced to meet an old man
> Clothed all in leather.
> He began to compliment
> And I began to grin:
>   "How do you do?"
> And "How do you do?"
> And "How do you do?" again.

> Once a child has these sounds clearly and solidly in his ear,
> he has little difficulty reading this old rhyme
> in its printed form.
> Once his ears begin telling him
> what his eyes are seeing,
> he approaches the reading with confidence and
>   expectation.*

Eve Merriam, a distinguished writer and teacher of writing who has received the National Council of Teachers of English Award for the excellence of her many volumes of poetry for children, insists that children and poetry do indeed form a *natural* partnership. Poetry's musical effects of rhyme, rhythm, and alliteration—extensions of children's own speech—naturally appeal to them. Like poets, children are intrigued by the marvelous things words can do: how sounds mimic what is being described, how puns are possible, how language can be made, in Eve Merriam's words, to "natter, patter, chatter and prate."†

In talking about children and poetry, Eve Merriam emphasizes the physical aspect of experiencing: "I try to give young people a sense of the sport and playfulness of language, because I think it's like a game. There's a physical element in reading poetry aloud; it's like jumping rope or throwing a ball."‡ She advises aspiring poets not to intellectualize but to respond to words with movement, the *natural* way: "Use your whole body as you write. It might even help sometimes to stand up and move with your words."

Out Loud is both the title of a volume of her verse and also Eve Merriam's teaching philosophy in two words. Reading aloud again

---

*Bill Martin, Jr., *Sounds of a Distant Drum,* Teacher's ed. (New York: Holt, Rinehart & Winston, 1967), p. 3.
†Eve Merriam, "Gab," in *Out Loud* (New York: Atheneum, 1974), p. 4.
‡Quotations from Eve Merriam in this and the following paragraph are from Glenna Sloan, "Eve Merriam," *Language Arts,* vol. lviii (November/December 1981), pp. 957–64.

and again "lets the music of the language sink in. If we can get teachers to read poetry, lots of it, out loud to children, we'll develop a generation of poetry lovers; we may even have some poetry writers, but the main thing, we'll have language appreciators."

Hearing verse, speaking it, moving to it is the best way to learn to read and write. For in the verse the child hears echoes of his own speech patterns and feels in his bones rhythms that his body recognizes. Of course, listening to poetry will not by itself teach a child to write. Plenty of practice with appropriate guidance is part of the process (as we shall discuss later). But, as in the development of interest in reading, poetry and other imaginative literature are natural and necessary prerequisites for writing. If we impose alien structures too soon—expecting a child to write practical prose with the mechanical accuracy of a business executive or computer print-out—our efforts are doomed to failure. Starting where the child is means knowing where he is and acknowledging it. The prose route to literacy is a rough one as teachers will testify who have to listen to pedestrian basal-reader prose haltingly read and peruse prose offerings that are like essays in a foreign language imperfectly learned.

In the drive toward literacy, we have splintered the subject "English" into a number of discrete entities: reading, listening, speaking, writing, spelling, grammar—each with its own textbooks, drills, exercises, and timetable slots. Reading in particular has often been divorced from the rest of the "language arts," sometimes taught to children by teachers who teach them no other language activity. New knowledge from linguistics and literary criticism indicates the folly of this fragmented approach to language studies. English conceived of in terms of just two components, language and literature, is recognized as a more viable, more holistic, concept. With younger children we are probably best advised to think of English in terms of literature since their intellectual development is largely pre-logical and concerned with imaginative rather than discursive forms of thought. Certainly the fragmented approach to language study has not been particularly effective. It may even be a dangerous and destructive deception, since the view of English as a collection of "communication skills" carries with it the assumption that discursive prose is the point of departure for language learning.

Yet scholars like Ernst Cassirer, Edward Sapir, and Otto Jesperson have confirmed that the essence of language is not communication. The egocentric speech of children is one indication that the purely communicative aspect of language has been exaggerated.

Language in the young is as likely to be expressive as utilitarian. Children delight in the repetition of words and phrases for their musicality, even when their meaning eludes them. Children use language as much for its affectiveness as its effectiveness.

Some years ago, a film was made telling the story of Victor, an adolescent captured in 1799 in southern France, where for years he had roamed like an animal, savage and mute. A young doctor Itard undertook the boy's education. Acting on the assumption that language is produced primarily to serve practical ends, he struggled to teach Victor to communicate efficiently. The project was eventually abandoned and judged unsuccessful for a number of reasons. Among them was Dr. Itard's failure to realize how Victor used language. The child, for example, never used the word *lait* to obtain milk but only to express his pleasure *after* the enjoyment of it. Indeed, the few spoken words Victor did master were spoken only when he contemplated their objects with joy or sorrow, not when he lacked anything.

In childhood the conception of reality is subjective and dreamlike. Practical associations and all the trappings of reason develop later, toward adolescence. The child grasps analogies that more experienced and practical minds reject as absurd. His mind and senses create relationships foreign to practical thinking. Our advanced society places great value on the practical, prosaic, discursive mode of language and thought. We begin to believe that language began as a utility, that metaphors are merely distortions of fact. Children are not so easily misled. They resist factual prose by refusing to read and write it. They are themselves poets and storytellers, and thrive best on poems and stories.

Experiencing language through all the senses is how a literary education ought to begin. Language must be absorbed from top to toe, not by the head alone. Only then can what we write emerge from the depths of personality, as an expression that is truly personal. Sylvia Ashton-Warner, in her efforts to help her Maori pupils toward literacy, discovered the significance to children of the affective aspects of language. "First words must have intense meaning for a child," she writes in *Teacher*.

> They must be part of his being. How much hangs on the love of reading, the instinctive inclination to hold a book. *Instinctive.* That's what it must be. The reaching out to hold a book must be an organic action. . . . Words must be organically born from the dynamic life itself. . . . First books must be made of the stuff of the child himself, whatever and wherever the child.*

*Sylvia Ashton-Warner, *Teacher* (New York: Bantam Books, 1964), p. 30.

For Sylvia Ashton-Warner's pupils, written expression in the words of their key vocabularies was stimulated by dancing, because their teacher understood that the two rhythms were intimately related. Children have always known how language and movement relate. They bounce balls in time to words, they skip to chants, they tease with taunting rhythmic rhymes. They know the powerful magic of incantation:

> White horse, white horse,
> Bring me good luck;
> Good luck to you,
> Good luck to me,
> Good luck to everyone I see.

The linguistic stuff of the child is not all practical and prosaic, nor logical and utilitarian. It begins in babbling for the sheer joy of it. It continues in the rousing repetitions of polysyllabic mouthfuls used by two-year-olds as rhythmic background for table beating and pan pounding. And for the child, language is as basic and as rhythmic as his body language and as inextricably bound to it— until, in school, we chain him to his seat and insist that he use only his mind in becoming literate.

Literature and the Development of Literacy

In the introduction to *The Acts of King Arthur and His Noble Knights,** John Steinbeck writes:

> Some people there are, who being grown, forget the horrible task of learning to read. It is perhaps the greatest single effort that the human undertakes, and he must do it as a child. . . . For a thousand thousand years humans have existed and they have only learned this trick—this magic—in the final ten thousand of the thousand thousand. . . . I remember that words—written or printed—were devils, and books, because they gave me pain, were my enemies. . . . Books were printed demons—the tongs and thumbscrews of outrageous persecution. Then one day, an aunt gave me a book and fatuously ignored my resentment. I stared at the black print with hatred, and then, gradually the pages opened and let me in. The magic happened.

The book his aunt gave Steinbeck was a cut version of the

*John Steinbeck, *The Acts of King Arthur and His Noble Knights* (New York: Farrar, Straus & Giroux, 1976), pp. xi–xii.

Caxton *Morte d'Arthur* of Thomas Mallory. Steinbeck continues,

> I loved the old spelling of the words and the words no longer used. Perhaps a passionate love of the English language opened to me from this one book. . . . The very strangeness of the language dyd me enchante, and vaulted me into an ancient scene.

A similar story is likely to be found in the biography of every writer. Adult writers at every level, from Pulitzer Prize winners to editors of local newspapers, acknowledge the role of reading in making them writers. Early acquaintance with favorite books instilled in them a passionate love for written words, their own and those of others. The truly literate are those who know from experience the power of written words, because these have made a difference in their lives.

As Andrew Wilkinson says in *The Foundations of Language,* "Many people do not feel a need to develop their language, and the reason is that they are unaware of the possibilities of language. They imperfectly appreciate the nature, the uses and the joy of language."* Only from literature, art in words, can children begin to learn about the nature, the uses, and the joy of language.

Forty prominent authors were asked for their advice in improving the writing of young students.† From those who responded, among them five recipients of Pulitzer Prizes, came a clear message: read to write.

"The urge to write is the child of the love of reading," wrote John Hersey. From Mary Stolz: "I have never known or known of a writer who was not a reader from the first dazzling moment when the letters assembled themselves and became the WORD." William Styron said, "The only absolutely indispensable factor in the teaching of writing is, it seems to me, an insistence on the necessity of *reading.*"

These are the words of Elizabeth George Speare, twice winner of the Newbery Award for her distinguished contribution to literature for young people:

> How wonderful if we could present a young writer with an intriguing Lego set of words with which to fit together his thoughts! On second thought, we do have just such a treasure, an inexhaustible

---

*Andrew Wilkinson, *The Foundations of Language* (New York: Oxford University Press, 1971), p. 139.

†Donald R. Gallo, ed., *Teaching Writing: Advice from the Professionals, Connecticut English Journal,* vol. viii (Spring 1977), entire issue.

Lego set of words. We have books. Our greatest advantage is our own love for them, and encouraging children to read is our responsibility and delight. I would also like to make a special appeal for reading aloud.

The emotional impact of a well-written story or poem, read aloud, can be profound. It may well be the Goose Bump Experience that leads a child to a love of carefully crafted language, a love that will last a lifetime. At seven, Henry James, hiding under a table to listen to a chapter of *David Copperfield* read by a relative, was discovered and sent to bed when he burst into tears at the cruelty of the Murdstones. Novelist Walker Percy remembers his father reading *The Jungle Book* and *Treasure Island* aloud to him: "To this day I remember certain passages from Kipling and every concrete detail of the way he read them." Donald Barthelme has a vivid recollection of being read to as a child, one book in particular whose title he can't recall: "I've been searching for that book all my life. The feeling of it, the tone, I remember: the music, but not the words." Those familiar with the cadences of Dylan Thomas's poetry will not be surprised to learn that his father, a grammar school teacher, read him Shakespeare and only Shakespeare from the time he was a toddler.* Poet Eve Merriam acknowledges that certain favorite poems, like the parodies of Mother Goose by Guy Wetmore Carryl and his brother Charles, directly influenced her own writing.†

Although the informal, albeit unscientific, evidence is overwhelming that literacy develops out of early pleasurable experiences with fine literature, many educators choose to ignore it. Reading aloud is rarely a regular, planned activity in classrooms. Independent reading of good books for sheer enjoyment is seldom seen inside school. Preference there is usually given to instructional activities—directed reading lessons, phonics exercises, and the like—whose results are measurable, if not always significant or long-lasting.

Recently, however, educational researchers, particularly psycholinguists, have provided data about the importance of literature in developing literacy that give authority to the less scientific testimonials of poets and other writers. For example, studies of children who read early without formal instruction as well as those who respond well when they are first taught to read indicate that

*Quoted in Ralph Tyler, "Reading Aloud: Is It Time for a Revival?", *Bookviews*, vol. i (September 1977), pp. 16–20.
†Sloan, "Eve Merriam," p. 962.

certain factors are present in the backgrounds of nearly every early reader.*

> —These children are read to from an early age, often before they can understand what the reading voice is saying.
> —Books, magazines, and newspapers are available in their homes; their parents show by example that they value and enjoy reading.
> —Adults stimulate the children's interest in reading and writing by answering questions about what is read, praising a child's efforts to read or write, taking the child to the library regularly, buying books for the child's own library, displaying the child's paperwork, or writing stories that the child dictates.
> —Paper, pencils, and crayons are readily available for experiments in literacy by the child, beginning with scribbling and leading to an interest in copying letters.

Studies show that language development is affected by reading aloud to young children.† Reading aloud begun with children as young as thirteen months showed differences in infant speech favoring the experimental group after only four months of the experiment. The effectiveness of systematic reading of stories in aiding the language acquisition of two- and three-year-olds was demonstrated by the fact that they received higher scores on measures of vocabulary and sentence length than children in control groups. One researcher found that reading aloud to fourth, fifth, and sixth graders had a positive effect on their reading interests as well as their ability to comprehend.

If physically we are what we eat, then linguistically we are what we read and hear. In one study, the researcher found that the writing of children contained features of their reading texts.‡ This finding has important implications for teaching. Since what children read directly affects how they will write, models need to be carefully chosen. Well-told tales and carefully crafted poems on the

*Margaret Clarke, *Young Fluent Readers: What Can They Teach Us?* (London: Heinemann Educational Books, 1976); Dolores Durkin, *Children Who Read Early* (New York: Teachers College Press, 1966).

†Sandra McCormick, "Should You Read Aloud *to* Your Children?", *Language Arts,* vol. liv (February 1977), pp. 139–43.

‡Barbara Eckhoff, "How Reading Affects Children's Writing," *Language Arts,* vol. lx (May 1983), pp. 607–16.

child's level of comprehension are to be preferred over the thuds and thumps of graceless text book prose.

Stories in books, created by writers of talent, are often simple enough for beginning readers to read independently. Many of these contain the repetitive language patterns that children enjoy and that help them to predict what comes next. Examples are "The Gingerbread Boy," "The Little Red Hen," "The Three Billy Goats Gruff," Else Minarik's *Little Bear,* Ann McGovern's *Too Much Noise,* Ruth Krauss's *The Carrot Seed,* and Robert Kraus's *Leo, the Late Bloomer.* These are stories that repeat themselves with wit and charm, carrying readers along with their patterned flow of words. When it comes to charm, inventiveness, freshness of approach, and imaginativeness, there is no contest between literary language of distinction and textbook prose like the following, a passage from the SRA Reading Program:

THE TAN CAT AND THE FAT CAT

Al has a tan cat—Kit.
Kit, the tan cat, can sit.
Kit, the tan cat, can nap.
  Kit sat and had a nap.
A fat cat ran to Kit.
Kit ran to a pit.
  Kit sat at the pit.
The fat cat ran to the pit. . . .*

Until educators accept and act on the fact, now documented with empirical evidence, that literacy is developed through literature, we are in trouble as teachers of reading and writing. If we must have reading textbooks, let us insist that they be written by those already literate, containing stories and poems that appeal to the imagination and the emotions, that foster a child's sense of wonder, that evoke strong feelings, that express what a child may feel but cannot put into words. Let us open the best books and let them take the children in. Only the best can make the magic happen.

Literacy begins in hearts, not heads. For some it may begin in the moment of silent awe that follows the reading of a poem like "The Ballad of the Harp Weaver," by Edna St. Vincent Millay. For

---

*Donald Rasmussen and Lynn Goldberg, *A Pig Can Jig,* Basic Reading Series, Level A, Part 2 (Chicago: Science Research Assoc., 1976), pp. 6–7.

others it might start with laughter at the mishaps of Pooh and Piglet or in tears at Charlotte's death. For little ones, chanting the refrain of Wanda Gág's *Millions of Cats* might be all it takes. There is a story or poem to raise a goose bump on the toughest skin, and we are well advised to try to find it. A child who has never thrilled to words will remain indifferent to reading or writing them.

Literature and the Imagination

If literature is essential to the development of readers and writers who are genuinely literate, it is also essential to the education of the child's imagination. We have no standardized tests to measure imagination, but this does not mean that its education can be neglected. It is after all through the imagination that we participate in every aspect of our daily lives: in conversation, in relating to others with sympathy and consideration, in making choices and decisions, in analyzing news reports and the speeches of politicians, in evaluating advertisements and entertainment.

There is no definitive description of the imagination. But we know that this creative and constructive power is not exclusive with the artist or the inventor. Every individual has an imagination. It is not secondary to the intellect or the emotions; it is the very core of them. Its dual nature allows us to take and give, comprehend and create. Children listen with delight to rhymed riddles and create their own; the stories they hear and read are inspiration for original stories in words or pictures. Literature flows from literature.

How can the study of literature help us to imaginative awareness? Like all art it is concerned not so much with reproducing the world we live in as with creating a world we can imagine. Genuine literature is made up of works that are timeless because they deal with basic human concerns. They are full of life but are not necessarily lifelike. The imaginative reality of literature is heightened like action on a stage. Rhythms are more concentrated, imagery is bolder, conventions are more stylized and varied than anything we know in ordinary experience.

The writer of a story or poem constructs a world that is but never was; within each world is an endless range of imaginative possibilities. A story is not real life—anything can happen, anything goes. Literature illustrates something essential for human beings to realize: that there are no limits for the imagination. Literature makes carpets fly and rabbits talk; it overcomes the tyranny of time and conquers death itself. A Yellow Brick Road leading to an Emerald City will never be found on a road map, but it exists, along with other literary locations, as an imaginative reality.

Furthermore, literature has the capacity to develop our imaginative perspective on reality. What we call reality is a confusing tangle of experience: radios blare at us, advertisers bombard us, we are harassed and hurried, torn in a dozen directions. We have all had the desire, when the confusion of life is at its height, to "get away from it all," "to sort things out," "to see where we are," "to get ourselves together." We feel the need for some perspective on our fragmented experience. One way to get it is through the study of a wide variety of literature, the art that describes not what happens in the historical sense but what happens to human beings as they try to come to terms with living. *Literature gives shape to human experience.*

It also calls forth something from our own imaginative experience, something we "have always known" but couldn't express until literature put it into words and images for us. Thus literature puts us in touch with our own imaginative powers. Nothing is more important for creating a truly human world than realizing the power of our imagination. William Blake said that nothing is real beyond the imaginative patterns we make of reality. Imagination, in Blake's sense, *creates* reality. In the real world there can be no change or reform of any kind unless we first use our imaginations to describe what sort of world we want to build, the kind of life we want to lead.

All our beliefs and actions take shape around a social vision constructed by the imagination. Literature, verbal structures constructed by the power of the imagination, provides us with the means of comprehending and evaluating *all* the verbal structures that confront us: in textbooks, on television, in the speeches of politicians. Literature's use of words (as opposed to the use of words in propaganda) is disinterested. It presents cultural mythology—the important beliefs and concerns that inform our culture—with detachment.

The Adventures of Huckleberry Finn is "just a story" and we enjoy it for that. But it also reveals certain truths of American cultural mythology, history, and social life. What we believe in, what we say we believe in, what we believe is important—all our cultural mythology—is revealed in what are first and foremost good stories worth telling again and again. They express our myths: of the hero who conquered a wilderness with his axe and his gun, of the poor boy who achieves success through hard work, or our belief in continual progress toward "better" things. The myths that inform our culture exist in their purest forms in literature. They are there to be examined first as simple forms of human creativity.

Those who wish to influence others, for good or evil, make use of the same myths we find in literature: pastoral myths, hero myths, sacrificial myths, quest myths. The politician promises to take us back "to the good old days." The advertiser lures us with the promise of a vacation retreat "away from it all," or promises to make rugged heroes of those who eat the right breakfast food. The newspaper editorial shatters the reputation of one man to make a case for the political candidate it supports. The student who has encountered the genuine form of a myth in literature will be less likely to fall prey to its perverted form in the advertisement. He will recognize that the commercial showing the plain and unpopular girl suddenly made pretty and popular by the use of the right face cream is a version of the Cinderella story. He will know that an advertisement showing idealized young men and women kept happy, healthy, and forever youthful by drinking the right kind of cola has stolen its conventions from a literary form: the romance.

Such use of language and myth are part of a social mythology whose purpose is to persuade us to accept—usually for another's gain—the standards and values of the society in which we live. It provides a means of making us adjust to things as they are or as a profiteer would have us believe them to be. Some adjustment to our society is necessary, of course. But it is important to guard against too much passive acquiescence. We cannot fall prey to the illusions that society threatens us with, for example, those in propaganda, advertising, or entertainment.

The poet and storyteller on the other hand want nothing from us except a response from our imaginative worlds. Their poems and stories call forth imaginative response; they don't impose it from without. To be aware of one's imaginative social vision is to escape the prison of unconscious social conditioning. Genuine literature, although it may enlighten us, does not set out to teach or preach. Its structures are self-contained worlds that are detached from reality. In contemplating these worlds we develop a capacity for detachment. This capacity can then be carried over to everything in life that attempts to capture the imagination for whatever purpose. The reality of literature is an imaginative reality, surely the most important kind, for it corresponds to something within ourselves. It reminds us that we have an imaginative world of our own, a world of possibilities, that we are capable of freedom and of choice.

Young people require educated imaginations if they are to cope with the social pressures that confront them. A well-developed imagination is their protection against social mythology in all its forms: entertainment, advertising, propaganda, the language of cliche and stereotype, the abstractions of jargon and gobbledegook. In an irrational world the trained reason is important. But a developed imagination is fundamental to the survival of a sane society.

Chapter 2

A New Approach to Literature

Literacy is not something that occurs as the result of reading a book or two. Reading every book in the library will not guarantee the reader an educated imagination. The development of literacy and the education of the imagination through literature is a cumulative process resulting from a systematic and progressive study of literature. And the early study of literature must take its place in a continuum of study if the cumulative benefits of a literary education are to be realized.

The Need for Theory

Literature is widely considered to be primarily useful in supplying children with the sociological and psychological insights they need to interpret the world and survive in it. It is seen as a useful supplement to and aid in other learning such as social studies and science. The teaching of reading and the teaching of literature are generally regarded as entirely separate issues. The former is considered the proper major concern of the elementary school with literature functioning to stimulate interest in reading or to provide material for the practice of reading skills.

Indeed, there seems to be a widespread belief, originating perhaps with behaviorist psychology that has so long dominated the field of reading instruction, that children must be taught to read before they are introduced to real books. Most children, therefore, begin by reading made-up books, ironically called "readers."

It is widely believed that significant literary study is beyond the scope of younger students. The study of literature as an art, apparently conceived of as something onerous and pedantic, is held suspect by many who fear that the child's sense of wonder and delight in story and poetry are jeopardized if he is asked to consider his literary experiences as anything more than diversion.

This curious viewpoint suggests that study, like medicine, must be unpleasant to be effective. Even those who believe that the benefits of teaching literature are too important for it to be approached in a haphazard and unsystematic fashion are wary of teaching literature in the elementary school. Their unwillingness may be an indictment of their own educational experience in classrooms where the study of poems was really verse vivesection and the reading of a story signaled the assignment of a page of questions to be answered for homework. Their ambivalence may well be caused by problems of definition and interpretation.

What it means to "study literature" has long been an open question, not only in the elementary school but in high schools and colleges as well. There are almost as many approaches to the subject as there are teachers of it. Literature curricula are characteristically planned in *ad hoc* fashion: built around themes like survival or courage, developed chronologically, set up by periods or countries, or incorporated with other studies in the humanities. Although such approaches may have some validity, they are essentially piecemeal and haphazard and give students little sense of the unity of the study with a consequent loss of its impact.

The question of how literature should be taught to young children gives rise to more questions than answers. As one researcher put it:

> There is interest in the subject, but there are more questions than answers about objectives, content, and approaches for teaching literature in kindergarten through grade six. . . . The expression "teaching literature" is used relatively infrequently. . . . The broader, more general interpretations of literature in the elementary school expand into use of terms such as language, language arts, personal reading, individualized reading, interests and tastes, reading guidance, literature readers, appreciation, and variations of these.*

The fundamental concepts on which the study of literature might be based and upon which more advanced studies can later be built have not been given adequate consideration. The teaching

---

*Norine Odland, *Teaching Literature in the Elementary School* (Urbana, Ill.: National Council of Teachers of English, 1969), p. 1.

of literature suffers in comparison with science and mathematics from not having more theory of this kind—it is possible to educate the imagination as systematically as mathematics and science train the reason. It is as easy, if not easier, for a child to learn the meaning of rhythm, plot, or form as it is to learn the meaning of sets, area, or equivalent fractions.

It is time to abandon the *ad hoc* approach to this important area of study. There is no legitimate excuse for delaying significant instruction until a child comes of high school age. Young children are perfectly capable of genuine intellectual activity if it is tailored to their needs, interests, and level of intellectual achievement.

Children's literature must cast off its Cinderella rags. For too long it has been a servant in the classroom: used to teach reading skills, inculcate moral values, develop positive self-concepts, and/or provide insights into the history of other people and other lands. Of course it is true that literature is useful in doing all of these things and more. But literature is first of all an art and should be taught *as literature* for its own sake and for its own inherent values. Everything else associated with its study is of secondary consideration.

What "Teaching Literature" Means

When we refer to children as critics in the context of this book, it is only to suggest what they do when they study literature. What we teach and learn when we study literature is criticism. Criticism, which may have other meanings in different contexts, here refers to what happens when children "study" literature.

It is convenient to say that we teach and study literature. But literary works cannot be directly "taught" or "learned"; they are *experienced*. The experience of literature is not directly transmittable from one person to another. But the knowledge of what literature is and how it works *can* be taught.

What we teach and learn when we "study" literature is criticism—all the trappings used to talk about literature and to respond to it. This does not mean that the study of literature is indirect learning *about* literary works. The experiencing of poems and stories is obviously of primary importance, but it is not something that can be taught. Every individual has his own private and personal reaction to a work. It may excite, inspire, and delight him, but experience alone does not build up his knowledge of what literature is all about. Experiencing a city full of buildings is not studying architecture. Experiencing works of literature as discrete entities does not add to one's knowledge of literature as a whole, and gives no sense of the coherence of the subject.

There needs to be created, through criticism, a sense of the progressive and systematic, an awareness of the significance of literature that goes beyond the experiencing of individual works. Criticism is an approach to literature that gives shape and structure to experience: it is not esoteric; it should not conjure up pictures of scholars in ivory towers writing articles for learned journals. It is what happens anywhere literature is treated as an art.

Criticism begins in the experiencing of literature in all its forms, when, for instance, kindergarten children listen to a story or poem, delighting in it as an artistic entity. The process involves the child's learning to make a distinction between imaginative verbal structures and passages of factual discourse. It includes his learning to react to *the total structure* of a story or poem without necessarily trying to extract from it a Timeless Truth or Key Idea.

Comprehension of story content and form is part of criticism, with an emphasis on the affective and imaginative as well as on the cognitive aspects of comprehending. The teacher helps pupils grow in their ability to take in stories and poems as imaginative verbal constructs by asking questions specifically designed to foster literary understandings. Such questions are those that focus the child's attention on the elements of story as they interact in the shaping and structuring of the form of the literary work as a whole and not in bits and pieces of its content. They are questions that center, for example, not so much on what a character did and when he did it but on *why* he had to behave as he did to make his story happen.

The child's response to the literature he encounters is a central aspect of criticism. The response may come in the form of question or comment; it may involve sharing a favorite poem or retelling a familiar story; it may be an original composition in words, a drawing, a dramatization, a puppet play, a dance drama, or the story board for a film. In the attempt to guide and foster the child's growth in comprehension and responsiveness, a teacher guides responses, providing assistance in planning and structuring them, and opportunities for developing, sharing, and evaluating them.

Criticism includes comprehension of individual literary works considered *as* literature and the child's response to the work, but it does not end there. It continues with efforts to help the child unify and integrate all of his literary experiences, in and out of school, and gain a sense of the significance this art has for him.

Northrop Frye, the distinguished literary critic and an eminent professor at the University of Toronto, describes literature as the range of articulate human imagination from its heights to its depths, man's revelation to man. Criticism must lead to an awareness of the significance of that revelation. Students should eventually see that every work is part of this total structure or order of words created by the power of imagination. They should see, too, how literature is related to other works of the imagination.

It is this last component of criticism that provides for elementary literary criticism its place of significance in the continuum of literary studies. Children, with materials and methods appropriate to their level of maturity, can make a beginning in significant literary criticism. As they proceed through the levels of formal education, the basic understandings they have acquired will provide a foundation upon which more sophisticated understandings may be built. Through their consideration of the structural principles of literature, children are provided with a broader conception of what literature is. They are less likely, when they can fit isolated literary experiences into a pattern, to leave school thinking of literature as a collection of unrelated works, only some of which they enjoyed or remember, or regarding the study of literature as without application to their experiences out of school.

The study of literature—criticism—begins before kindergarten and continues through graduate school. The aim of the study is not to develop professional reviewers, scholars, or researchers. The aim is more fully developed human beings. Genuine criticism is a systematic study that treats literature as an art. It involves talking about literature in a way that will build up a systematic structure of knowledge *of* literature, taking the student beyond the subjectivity of his experience out into a wider, more comprehensive world.

How Children Develop as Critics

Children develop literary understandings when they are read to or read for themselves a variety of literature: Mother Goose rhymes, concept books, picture books, poetry, Bible stories, myths, legends, folktales, fables, fantasy, "realistic" stories, historical fiction, biography, and informational books. A wide experience with literature and with the subliterary world of television, comics, series books, and the mass media provides children with an enormous amount of literary knowledge. Of course, few children will realize what they know without help. It is through questioning and discussion that teachers, librarians, and other adults can get students to understand the significance of what they already know. (Examples of the kind of exchange that draws forth knowledge already absorbed through listening, reading, and viewing are found in Chapters 6 and 7 of this book.)

The kinds of literary understanding that children develop vary at different ages. The types of understanding typical of each age are listed below.

Preschool

—Learns about story and poetic forms through listening to stories and poems read as entities; learns to listen to stories and poems as wholes.
—Learns what books are and how they are used.
—Helps to "read" stories by joining in on repeated words and phrases.
—Is able to enter the story world the author creates.
—Follows story sequence through pictures.
—Learns that stories have shape: beginnings, middles, and ends.
—Insists on accuracy in retelling and rereading.
—Learns about character and plot through dramatic play.
—Begins to distinguish among different types of stories: make-believe (fantasy), stories about everyday life.
—Becomes selective, preferring some stories and poems over others.
—Learns to associate the tone of the reading voice with story content.
—Hears and repeats figurative and rhythmic language from books and television.
—Engages in readinglike behavior: holds books, turns pages, points to words and pictures, "reads" by retelling a story as it is remembered.

Primary Grades

—Can listen to longer, more complex stories and poems.
—Likely to ask more "Why?" questions about characters, plots, and, in particular, endings.
—Watches cartoons and stories on TV, recognizing stock characters (hunter, hunted) and basic plots (the chase).

—Anticipates what will come next in a story.

—Shows need for unity, coherence, and resolution in stories.

—Can categorize stories more precisely and group like stories together.

—Recreates stories and creates original ones through dramatic play, drawing, writing, or dictating.

—Repeats jingles and rhymes from TV advertising, appreciates language play in puns, riddles, and jokes.

—Can associate certain animals and settings with what is desirable and their opposites with what is undesirable. E.g., dogs are "good," weasels are not; it is better to be lost in a meadow than a forest.

—Begins to read independently, often choosing what was read aloud.

Middle Grades

—Reads independently and selectively; rejects stories as dull when they lack dramatic action and conflict.

—Recognizes that stories come in different shapes or forms: the quest, the struggle to overcome odds, the chase.

—Knows story types or genres one from another: folktale, myth, fable, fantasy, realism.

—Can understand and even use literary terms: *character, plot, suspense, flashback, point of view* (whether story is told in first or third person).

—Can relate one incident in a plot to another; recognizes foreshadowing (story clues of events to come).

—Can distinguish tone: humorous, ironic, solemn.

—Recognizes recurrent character types: hero, heroine, villain, minor supportive characters.

—Notes similarities among characters in different stories: "The nasty stepmother is a witch!"

—Recognizes the style of particular authors and prefers one over another.

—Becomes interested in who makes stories and how; enjoys reading about authors and meeting them; favorite question to authors, "Where do you get your ideas?"

Upper Grades

—Familiar with patterns of recurring images in literature and the sub-literary: for example, confusion and chaos contrasts with peace and serenity; light and calm with darkness and storm.

—Knows from experience that archetypes (images, patterns, conventions, symbols) from myth and folktale inform both modern literature and the sub-literature of TV commercials, comics, etc. E.g., godlike characters like the Jolly Green Giant; cars presented as divine chariots; transformations through the use of the right mouthwash, face cream, or floor cleaners.

—From experience, knows about allusion, word play, and metaphor, although unable to articulate this knowledge without help; enjoys poetry that abounds in word play; appreciates jokes, riddles, and puns; enjoys rhythmic language in TV commericals, popular song lyrics.

—Writes or draws stories featuring characters and plots met in reading, listening, and viewing; better able to resolve stories satisfactorily, if only by expedient means: character in a tight spot wakes up; the adventure was only a dream; an extraneous character is introduced to "save the day."

—Associates various literary experiences: stories read are compared to those seen on TV.

Value Judgments

Direct experience of literature is highly personal and subjective and is more likely to end with a value judgment than a literary judgment. Value judgments made about literature invariably reveal more of the evaluator than the work. They are generally statements about the immediate effect of a poem or story on a reader. Value judgments are subjective evaluations, reflecting a given individual's personality, experience, and predilections.

Questions to children about what they like or dislike are not only futile in the critical sense but likely to be inhibiting. Refinements of taste, desirable though they may be, result from prolonged experience with the widest possible variety of the art, and they cannot be taught by or caught from another except in the most superficial sense. The teacher who attempts "to teach good taste" does so at the risk of alienating young readers who, at a particular moment in their lives, may find Nancy Drew or the Hardy Boys the nonpareil of literary form. Their personal response, redeemed by honesty, should, like grief, be private and respected. They should not be placed in the position of having to admit what it is they most enjoy or abhor, since this is not what constitutes a genuine criticism of literature. What one likes, in any case, is often what one has experienced; the new or unusual is likely to be suspect.

The skilled teacher provides opportunities for broadening experience by introducing and making palatable and interesting a wide range of material and providing unlimited choice to satisfy a variety of tastes and preferences. The teacher's responsibility in matters of taste and judgment lies entirely with his ability to interest children in literature *of all kinds.* One of his finest qualities is his ability to refrain from expressing dismay at the personal preferences of the inexperienced. The teacher understands that the ability to evaluate is a by-product of genuine criticism and not its primary objective.

Genuine criticism is centered in knowledge rather than value judgments. It is more comparative than evaluative. It involves an effort by the student of literature to examine and interpret each work in terms of all the literature he knows.

Unifying Function of Criticism

Genuine criticism demonstrates that literature is a coherent order. It shows how each literary work is a part of that order and how nonliterary imaginative structures like advertisements, commercials, and popular songs are related to it. To accomplish this, criticism must be founded on a theory that defines the structural principles of literature. Without such theory criticism remains merely commentary, informed or otherwise, that seldom shows how literary works are fundamentally related.

Without a sense of structure it is impossible to see how things are related. Without an understanding of the structure of literature as a whole it is impossible to see how each separate work of literature relates to the whole.

Northrop Frye was the first to attempt a delineation of the structural principles of literature. He has provided a scheme that allows us to see all the phenomena literary criticism deals with as parts of a whole. His literary theory, set out in its most complete form in his *Anatomy of Criticism,* provides the means for a new approach to the study of literature at all levels. In the next two chapters this theory is interpreted and related specifically to children's literature.

Professor Frye's vision of the fundamental unity in literature began with his extensive study of the work of the eighteenth-century visionary and poet, William Blake. He found within Blake's symbolic structures a recurrent pattern—the myth of a world created, fallen, redeemed by divine sacrifice, and moving toward apocalypse and rebirth. In his study of Blake's symbolism, Frye saw evidence that suggested the existence of archetypes and organizing principles for the whole of Western literature. Frye's *The Great Code: The Bible and Literature,* the first of a projected two-volume work on biblical language, metaphor, myth, and typology, takes its title from Blake's comment that "the Old and New Testaments are the Great Code of Art."

While it does not supplant other critical methods, Frye's literary theory supplies an umbrella for them; when we look at literature from his point of view, we have a panoramic perspective, largely lacking in other approaches, that allows us some sense of the unity of all literature, a sense that does not come readily from critical methods that focus on individual works. Frye himself insists that there is room in literary studies for a variety of critical systems; what is unique in his own—and the reason why it is chosen as the focus of this book—is his picture of literature as a coherent whole.

Professor Frye sees a fundamental unity in literature. Literature as a whole he calls "one story," the quest myth: the quest of the human imagination for identity. The framework of all literature is a myth or archetypal story that goes like this: Once man lived in a paradisal garden or golden age in harmony with the universe. Man lost his perfect home, became alienated from nature and other men, and subject to time and death. The quest to recover the lost golden age is man's attempt to regain his human identity. It is the same goal sought by him as he tries to turn his environment into a human home.

The quest myth is central to all literature and suggests the critic's social function. If this central myth envisions the fulfillment of human desires, the establishment of the totally human society, criticism is the activity that can unite literature with society. This is done by interpreting and systematizing the vision of the artist and making it accessible to all, a humanistic study of immense importance.

Criticism, properly undertaken, is a study of how imagination works in the creation of art in words. In the process, the student's own imagination is developed and his capacity for vision enlarged. Criticism, properly undertaken, leads to a conception of literature as a coherent structure. With this conception comes awareness of its significance in one's own life, and in the lives of all.

Chapter 3

The Structural Principles
of Literature

Literature is more than a collection of unrelated poems and stories; the more we read the more obvious this becomes. Hercules and Superman were created centuries apart but they are recognizable as the same character type: the hero with magical powers. We find images like gardens and wastelands in the Old Testament and in the songs of folksingers. That love is more powerful than any evil or even death itself is a theme found in stories as different as "Beauty and the Beast" and *Charlotte's Web*. We recognize the shape of the romance story in ancient epics and in today's westerns. The "good" cowboy, remarkably like the knightly hero of old, goes forth with faithful horse and trusty weapon on a quest to rid the world of evil.

The recurring structural patterns of literature—characters, images, themes, story shapes, events, and symbols—are *archetypes*. They are fundamental patterns that occur again and again in the literature of all ages. Nor are these units of imaginative thought common only to the main body of literature, they turn up in comics and films, in advertisements, in the writings of children. The archetype of the establishment of a "rightful kingdom" we can find in such different places as John F. Kennedy's Inaugural Address, in the Greek myth of Perseus, and in the song "Aquarius" from the popular musical of the sixties, *Hair*. The idealized green and golden world of romance is a favorite archetype of advertisers, for who can resist a product when it is associated with beauty, youth, and good times in a world of forever-summer?

Archetypes are intuitive, timeless, and stable. In them are expressed all our basic human concerns: who we are, where we come

28

from, where we are going, how we should live. They are the concepts that give literature its unity.

The word *convention* expresses another kind of similarity we find in literature. If we read a detective story, for instance, we expect to find certain elements in it—a crime, someone to solve it, a criminal who is apprehended. Each detective story, like each game of chess or checkers, is different enough from others to make it a distinct experience, yet similar enough to make us recognize it as one of a type. In addition, we find that literary works fall into categories or genres. We expect a comedy to have certain features that a tragedy will not have. Comedies, in general, turn "up" at the end; tragedies turn "down."

The content of each story is unique, just as each infant is a unique human being. But, just as a baby is recognizably a member of the human race, stories are recognized by the various recurrent patterns within them as members of the whole family of literature. Literature grows out of other literature, deriving its forms from itself. And every form or pattern in literature has a pedigree. We can trace its descent back to the earliest times.

Literary Patterns from Mythology

From its beginnings literature has been man's imaginative attempt to give shape, order, and structure to his experience. It began with myth and ritual, the myth being the spoken part of a ritual, the story that the ritual enacts. Early religious rituals aimed at securing the well-being of a people and all shared the same general pattern: they depicted the death and resurrection of a god-king in a series of episodes that typically included a battle in which the god-king was victorious, a triumphal procession, an enthronement, a ceremony to ensure the destinies of the people for the coming year, and a sacred marriage.

Confronted with an alien universe, man, the storytelling animal, described natural phenomena in human terms. Occurrences in nature that frightened and bewildered him were given human shapes and "controlled" through story by means of analogy and metaphor. The clearest forms of such associations are in mythical images where we have "gods" who are human in shape and character, yet identified with something in nature like the sun or the seasons. The successful completion of a god-king's ritual quest signified human control over the natural world.

Feeling lost and helpless against the forces of nature, early man told stories of a time when he and nature were in harmony.

The story of the Garden of Eden is one such story but similar ones are to be found in the mythology of many cultures. The story tells how man lost his perfect home, became alienated from the rest of the universe, and subject to time and death. By the power of his imagination man seeks to regain the lost perfect world. In later stories—legends and folk tales—the gods take on more human characteristics and have less divine power. Eventually they disappear from stories and characters become more and more recognizable as limited human beings. Even so, there always exists the desire, expressed in poems, stories, and even in the lyrics of a popular song, to "get back to the garden." Our literature is a continuous journal of man's search for identity, a metaphorical quest to rediscover a lost perfection. In modern literature nature is no longer a threat, but the world often seems an alien place, and stories still tell of the individual's efforts to find a place in it.

For constructing any work of art you need some principle of repetition or recurrence, like rhythm in music and pattern in painting. In the early development of literature from myth, the story-teller took for his recurring pattern the cycles of nature and eventually made analogies between the natural cycles and the human life cycle.

Mythologies are filled with tales of young gods or heroes—Perseus, Theseus, Hercules—who go through various successful adventures, endure great dangers, are deserted, betrayed, even killed, but who usually emerge safely in the end. The movement of the stories is analogous to the progression of the seasons or of the sun across the sky. The merging of the natural cycle with mythology provided myths with two opposing movements: the rising movement that we find in myths of birth, marriage, and resurrection; and the falling movement in myths of death, metamorphosis, or sacrifice. Later these movements appear as the rising movement of comedy and the falling movement of tragedy.

These early stories reveal another aspect of man's imagination. The hero's quest also involves a dialectical or philosophical way of looking at life, reflecting at one limit what man most desires and at the other what he most hates and fears. Myths project a paradise above the world of experience, a place of wish-fulfillment in which all obstacles are overcome. Below it, they project a hell, a world of nightmare and bondage. To the quest for identity, then, is added this goal: the possession of a state where man is released from an indifferent world into the upper world of his dreams, a world that is the opposite of his nightmares. These two opposing worlds appear in literature as the idealized world of romance and the absurd, suffering, frustrated world of irony and satire (as illustrated in figure 3.1 and amplified in tables 3.1 and 3.2).

Out of the cycle of death and renewal and man's emotional response to it there gradually emerged the four fundamental themes of imaginative experience: 1) romance, 2) tragedy, 3) comedy, 4) irony-satire. In romance we see how strong and beautiful heroes and heroines set out in search of the ideal green and golden world, the world of forever-summer. Tragedy tells how man, although he is capable of great things, has limited powers. He is sometimes a victim of forces he doesn't understand and cannot control. Just as the autumn leaves must fall so he must inevitably move toward his death. Irony and satire present the wintry world

FIGURE 3.1.   Literary Imagery

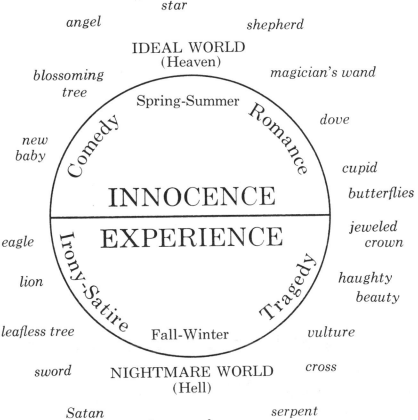

TABLE 3.1. Images of Heaven and Hell

	Heavenly	Demonic
Divine images	Benevolent gods "above" Luck Angels	Malicious gods "below" Blind fate Devils

Sky images	Sunlight
	Angels
	
	Promethean fire
		Darkness
		Demons and pestilence
		  (as released from
		  Pandora's box)

Human images	Humans as community, members of one body The Good Shepherd	Humans as mindless mob The tyrant
Animal images	Lamb, dove	Monsters, birds and beasts of prey
Vegetable images	Garden of Paradise Tree of Life	Wilderness Gallows
Water images	Water of Life	Flood
Mineral images	Temple Jacob's ladder The One Way	Wasteland Tower of Babel The labyrinth

TABLE 3.2. Images of Innocence and Experience

	Innocence	Experience
Divine images	Good parents Wise old men Fairy godmothers	False fathers and wicked stepmothers Wizards and sorcerers Witches and hags
Sky images	Staff, wand Moon and stars Spirits and fairies	Fiery sword, bombs Jewels and other treasure Hobgoblins

Human images	Loving siblings
	
	Wise and helpful men
	  and women
		Wicked stepsisters and
		  stepbrothers
		Witches, wizards,
		  temptresses

Animal images	Domesticated animals: dogs, sheep, horses Unicorns and dolphins	Birds and beasts of prey Lions and eagles
Vegetable images	Blossoming tree Magician's wand or staff Meadows	Dead tree King's scepter Gardens and parks
Water images	Warm rain Water as purifier	Sleet Water as destroyer
Mineral images	Paths Country Mountaintop	Highways City Subterranean tunnel

of experience where life is often as harsh and cruel as the winter winds. In comedy we find hopeful stories of the renewal of the human spirit. New life springs up as new growth comes again in the spring. Just as the seasons may be considered as distinct though related, so the four imaginative patterns may be seen as parts of the "one story," man's collective imaginative efforts to give shape to all of human experience.

John Keats's "The Human Seasons" is only one of many literary examples showing how "the mind of man" relates nature's cycles to his own life:

> Four seasons fill the measure of the year;
>   There are four seasons in the mind of man:
> He has his lusty Spring, when fancy clear
>   Takes in all beauty with an easy span:
> He has his Summer, when luxuriously
>   Spring's honied cud of youthful thought he loves
> To ruminate, and by such dreaming high
>   Is nearest unto heaven: quiet coves
> His soul has in its Autumn, when his wings
>   He furleth close; contented so to look
> On mists in idleness—to let fair things
>   Pass by unheeded as a threshold brook.
> His has his Winter too of pale misfeature,
> Or else he would forego his mortal nature.*

These two thought constructs (the cycle, together with the image of an upper ideal world and its opposite) underlie all of literature. Even a brief lyric poem, although it does not tell a "story," may express the emotions connected with the comic, spring part of the cycle or those related to the wintry world of irony. Because it is so structured, literature is in itself a coherent unity. Within this essentially simple structure one can fit all one's literary experiences. Each poem and story takes on a greater significance for it may be seen as part of a whole. The whole is the art of literature, man's imaginative attempt to make sense of the world and his existence in it.

The literature of every culture is shaped by its mythology. The Bible and classical mythology supply Western literature with the structure that informs it. The Old and New Testaments of the Bible together provide us with the most complete form we have of the

---

*H. W. Garrod, ed., *Keats: Poetical Works* (London: Oxford University Press, 1956), p. 423.

archetypal story of the loss and recovery of identity, the story that is the framework of our literature. The Old Testament begins with the story of the creation of man (Adam) in paradise, then goes on to tell of his fall from innocence and the loss of his original home. Eventually the story of Adam becomes the story of Israel, a people who endure a long exile in a wilderness where they cannot feel at home, and who quest to reestablish the ideal world—the rightful kingdom—they once knew here on earth. The New Testament tells of the coming of the second Adam (Christ), who rescues the human race from the wilderness and restores the lost paradise where man is at one with himself and God. The classical myths give us more clearly than does the Bible the main episode of the central myth of the hero whose mysterious birth, triumph, betrayal, death, and rebirth follow the rhythm of the seasons. All stories in literature are developments of fundamental shapes that are seen most clearly in myths, particularly the myth that tells of the quest of the hero.

Our literature is actually a series of "displacements" from the level of pure myth (religion) to naturalism or realism, the mode of most serious fiction in Western literature for the past hundred years. (Literature for children, until recently comic or romantic, is now increasingly being written in the realistic mode.) The images, themes, characters, and plots are "displaced" to make them rationally credible and acceptable to a particular audience, a point that becomes clear when we consider literature both historically and in terms of the principal character's powers of action.

At the level of pure myth we have characters who are divine, supernatural figures superior to men and nature. Next come the heroes of epics who are superior in degree to other men and to their environments, moving in a world where the ordinary laws of nature are suspended, and often in close touch with the gods themselves. The next level features princes, kings, and noblemen who are portrayed as superior to other men but not to their environment. At the next remove, the hero has powers similar to our own. The farthest displacement from myth is the ironic-satiric mode where we find the anti-hero who is inferior in power even to ordinary men, a victim of others and the powers of nature.

These levels may be traced through a linear progression in history, one mode dominating in a given period, though not to the exclusion of all other modes. Myth, for instance, prevailed from prehistory to the Middle Ages. Here we have Greek and Roman myths and later those of the Christians. Romance, featuring towering figures like King Arthur and his knights, dominated from the Middle Ages to the Renaissance. The "high mimetic" mode, to use

Frye's term, was dominant from the Renaissance to about 1700; the period includes Shakespeare's great tragic plays about the life of kings and princes like Lear and Hamlet. Dominant from 1700 to about 1900 was the "low mimetic" mode, most clearly seen in novels like those of Charles Dickens, which feature ordinary people who cope, mostly satisfactorily, with the problems of ordinary life. Since 1900, the ironic mode, early exemplified by the novels of Thomas Hardy, has dominated adult fiction.

In children's literature, which began to appear as separate and distinct from adult literature toward the end of the nineteenth century, the low mimetic mode prevailed until after 1950. Examples of the mode are stories of everyday experiences of ordinary folk by such authors as Louisa May Alcott and Lucy M. Montgomery, followed by Laura Ingalls Wilder, Elizabeth Enright, and Eleanor Estes.

Since 1950, realistic stories for children increasingly have incorporated many of the ironic elements common to adult fiction. Themes and subjects previously thought unsuitable for children's books are presented with candor: the fallibility of parents—*Queenie Peavy*, by Robert Burch; psychological problems—*(George)*, by E. L. Konigsburg; racism—*Mary Jane*, by Dorothy Sterling; drug addiction—*Turned Out*, by Maia Wojciechowska; illegitimacy—*Mom, the Wolf Man, and Me*, by Norma Klein; divorce—*Ellen Grae*, by Vera and Bill Cleaver.

Besides ironic realism for children, the contemporary literature features historical fiction (*The Bronze Bow*, by Elizabeth George Speare) and fantasy (*The Dark Is Rising*, by Susan Cooper; *A Wrinkle in Time*, by Madeleine L'Engle). These two forms permit protagonists the positive heroic action associated with romance and comedy.

Most writers for children, and their publishers, appear unwilling to rob children's literature of its role in educating the young in the positive social and moral ideals of society. In the main, literature for children continues to portray romantic and comic visions of life, where hope and optimism prevail.

Cyclical and Dialectical Imagery

The archetypal structures that underlie literary imagery are of two kinds: cyclical (imagery based on natural cycles) and dialectical (images that present contrasting worlds). Over and over in literature, images of the cycles of nature recur. Countless stories involve a cyclical journey, the hero or heroine returning in the end to the point of departure after a quest is completed. The pattern of the cyclical journey is common to tales old and new: Odysseus's story shows it, as does *The Tale of Peter Rabbit* and modern fantasies like *Where the Wild Things Are.*

Often associations are made between human and animal life and the daily or seasonal cycles. The rejected Ugly Duckling suffers his greatest loneliness in the winter when the ground is frozen and barren. He finds his identity in the springtime in a garden where apple trees are in bloom and the scent of lilac is in the air. When the Norse god Balder lies dead in Asgard, darkness spreads over heaven and earth, the "night of death." Johnny Appleseed dies but he is memorialized each spring when the apple trees bloom. In Robert Frost's "Stopping by Woods on a Winter Evening" the temptation to give up is associated with winter and the darkest evening of the year. In "Old Man and the Beginning of the World," a myth of the Blackfeet Indians, Old Man promises to return like the sun as he disappears into the west. In more westerns than we can count, the hero rides off into the sunset, not to die but to be reborn in yet another episode of his endless story. The epic hero Gilgamesh, in his quest to find the secret of life and death, follows the "way of the sun" to the Eastern Garden, the sun's dwelling.

Spring and summer are associated frequently with new beginnings, with joy and hope, youth and the prime of life. Autumn and winter are as often associated with old age, death, decay, and loss.

Above and below the world of man's experience, myth projects an upper, desirable ideal world (the heaven of religion) and its opposite, an undesirable nightmare state (hell). The main body of literature is not religious, however, and does not deal with heaven and hell. The human experience is seen as analogous to these contrasting worlds. William Blake called these human worlds *innocence* and *experience.* The imagery of the heavenly world reaches down into the world of innocence; that of the demonic, up into the world of experience (refer to figure 3.1). The heavenly world gives us images of gods like Zeus and the Oympians, a sky-father like Odin, the three-in-one god of the Christian religion. The demonic world is peopled with malicious gods like Satan, revealed through images of menacing natural forces like the sea in Armstrong Sperry's *Call It Courage,* or is represented by a blind fate against which man has no defenses. The tragic deaths of young innocents like Nadia in Jaap Ter Haar's *Boris* and Raidy in *The Loner* by Ester Weir are examples of imagery of the latter type.

The innocent world is one of romance, or of stories and poems with a comic or upward movement. Here good parents, wise old men, and benevolent fairy godmothers are analogous to the divinities of the heavenly world; false fathers, wicked stepmothers, and ambitious kings, to the undesirable gods of the demonic world. King Arthur's mentor, Merlin, and Chiron, instructor of Greek heroes like Achilles and Jason, are good examples of the wise old men who counsel the young. The cruel stepmother of "Snow White" and the vicious witch who captures Hansel and Gretel are typical of the heartless hags and other varieties of horrible women whose images haunt the tragic, ironic, sad visions of life. In a modern story, Julia Cunningham's *Dorp Dead*, the evil Kobalt is a literary relative once-removed from the wicked sorcerers and wizards of old fairy tales who are themselves one step away from the gods of the underworld. The hunter in the same book who befriends young Gilly provides an opposite image: that of counselor and benefactor. The story takes place in the human sphere but in the character of the hunter is an image that resembles the benevolent deity of the heavenly world.

Sky images come "down" and "up" from the heavenly and demonic worlds into the literary worlds that deal with human concerns. It becomes clear that knowledge of biblical and classical imagery will make the reading of all subsequent literature more richly meaningful. In the heavenly sphere we have the sun and the angels, the thunder of Zeus, and Prometheus's gift of the gods' fire to man. At the opposite pole is Lucifer and images of fire and brimstone. In between the world of fire may be one of malignant demons like the will-o'-the-wisp in tales old and new. In the innocent world fire is usually a purifying symbol, a world of flame that none but the pure may pass through. Sigurd, alone of all the Volsungs, is able to penetrate the wall of fire that surrounds Brynhild. In the story of the Sleeping Beauty the wall of fire is replaced by one of thorns and brambles, but the images are closely related. In the world of experience the heavenly fire blazes in the jewels of the king's crown and the flashing eyes of the beautiful lady.

Human images in the heavenly world are those of mankind as members of one body, united in God. At the beginning of the eighth book of the Iliad, Zeus remarks that, should he desire to do so, he can pull up the whole chain of being, both gods and humans, into himself, the supreme divine will. There are images of the Good Shepherd, pastor of a human flock. In the demonic world the human images indicate disorder and ruthlessness. Among them are cruel tyrants who demand human sacrifices, bloodthirsty mobs, and sirens like those in the Odyssey who tempt men to forget their humanity. In the world of innocence that we see in romance, kings and lords abound, analogous to the gods of heaven. Here the peasant and commoner are idealized, with poor but worthy lads like Boots meeting success against all odds.

In more "realistic" stories in the world of experience there is more relationship in imagery to the demonic world. Order and reason and justice do not prevail as in the innocent worlds of comedy and romance. Characters are common and typical men and women subject to all the ills that beset mankind. Here characters are more likely to be victims than triumphant heroes. The boy and his family in William Armstrong's *Sounder*, the young escapee from the concentration camp in Anne Holm's *North to Freedom*, and the lonely young orphan in Ester Weir's *The Loner* are examples.

Animal imagery in the innocent world strongly reflects the biblical and classical. Domesticated animals, notably the sheep, are symbols of devotion and loyalty, analogous to the Lamb of God. The dove and other gentle birds provide images of peace and love. Unicorns and dolphins contrast with the dragons and monsters of the demonic world. In the Bible we have the monster Leviathan, symbolic of the whole fallen world of sin, tyranny, and death in which man lives. Traditional tales like those of St. George and Beowulf commonly show the heroes fighting evil in the form of dragons and monsters.

Vegetable imagery in the heavenly world is well known to us. Both the Bible and classical mythology tell of gardens of paradise. The tree of life contrasts with the demonic cross. In the human worlds of innocence and experience, enchanted gardens and beautiful parks are just once removed from heavenly gardens. In romance pastoral settings like Sherwood Forest are desirable images. Many modern realistic stories with harsh, bleak urban settings show by contrast that the rural setting is still seen as closer to man's vision of the ideal. A romantic counterpart to the tree of life appears in the wand of the magician and the fairy godmother, which can provide life and miraculous change.

Demonic imagery is lacking entirely in lush vegetation. Hell is a rocky wasteland where no trees and plants grow. Its counterpart in modern stories of human experience is the concrete and glass city, often depicted as a place of alienation and despair, as in Paula Fox's *How Many Miles to Babylon* and Mary Weik's *The Jazz Man*.

In the Bible we have images of temples and jeweled cities paved with gold. These are reflected in the enchanted castles, courts, and capital cities of romance, and are frequently the goal of young travelers who journey on the highroad in search of treasure or a better life. The highroad itself may be seen as the counterpart of "the one way" of biblical imagery.

Water imagery extends all the way from the water of life to the Deluge. In romance literature the hero often descends into or under water just as the soul of biblical imagery sinks into it at death. For the hero of romance a descent into water may be a kind of ritual death. Mafatu in Armstrong Sperry's *Call It Courage* emerges from submersion in the sea reborn with a new identity. Water in the world of innocence may be symbolic of growth and fertility or seen, like the biblical ritual of baptism, as a purifier. King Midas must bathe himself in a pool to remove the stigma of the golden touch.

Dominic by William Steig shows how a contemporary writer for children makes use of conventional imagery. The hero is Dominic, a cheerful, gregarious mutt who leaves home to seek his fortune, to find adventure and a more satisfying life. Along the way he encounters his adversaries, the evil Doomsday Gang: foxes, weasels, ferrets, a wildcat, a wolf, tomcats, dingoes, and rats. The hero and those he befriends in the course of his travels are gentler animals, friendly to man and not given to preying on each other. Another friend is the helpful and wise woman in the form of an alligator witch. She shares her magic powers with him by giving him her wand in the shape of a sword that will make him invincible in combat.

Dominic sets out upon his adventures along a springtime road strewn with leafy trees and flowers. In the story the forest is the setting for the hero's greatest trials, confusion, and despair. It is only with great difficulty that Dominic is able to "get out of the woods" to safety. He finds treasure both in the form of diamonds, rubies, and emeralds and in someone to love. His love he discovers in a miniature palace in a beautiful enchanted garden where it is always summer. His dreams of a new and more fulfilling life have come true.

An examination of poetry written by children indicates that they have an intuitive grasp of these basic patterns of poetic imagery. Just as their first grasp of these patterns in what they read and hear is intuitive, so it is when they write to order their feelings and impressions. The following poems are all taken from *Poetic Composition Through the Grades* by Robert A. Wolsch. In the first example loneliness is associated with the cold wind of autumn:

>Child lonely playing
>In the cold and growling wind
>Sees a lone leaf drift.

In another, a child expresses a happy wish of flying high to a dance in the sky:

>If I could fly
>I'd roar through the sky
>So high! So high!! So high!!!
>I'd do all kinds of tricks
>I would! I would!
>I'd dance in the sky with all the birds,
>And when the day is over
>I'd rest on a silver white cloud.
>Wouldn't you
>Do that too?
>If you
>Could fly?!
>Fly!!!!!

The happy freedom of the flying bird contrasts with the sadness of the earthbound boy who is cheered by the bird who joins him to walk "on the dirt road" that is the boy's natural home:

>A beautiful bird
>   flew in the sky
>   and
>A sad little boy
>   sitting in the sand.
>   then
>The beautiful bird
>   flew on his shoulder
>   and
>   sang to him
>   and
>   the sad little boy
>   happy again
>   and
>   they both walk
>   on the dirt road.

Natural phenomena are seen as predatory animals:

> The darkening clouds,
> Blot out the sky,
> Thunder roaring like hungry tigers,
> Searching for their prey.
>   . . .

A conscious knowledge of the archetypal patterns of imagery will bring shape and focus to the child's own writing. Discussion of the symbols and images he will use to express ideas, wishes, dreams, nightmares, and the like will inform his own writing and enlighten his appreciation and understanding of the writing of others.

Taken together, the patterns of imagery and the narrative plots give us a structural framework within which all literary works will be found to have a place. This is not to say that every poem, play, and story should be prodded and pared until it fits into a slot. The framework simply provides us with an *organizational scheme* that enables us to see literature as a whole rather than as a collection of unrelated entities. Seeing literature as a whole allows us to feel its full imaginative impact and to recognize the ultimate power of the human imagination. This awareness should come to the student through a process of discovery. It will do no good to *tell* young students what the structural patterns of literature are. They must find them out for themselves. The framework is for teachers to use when structuring learning experiences designed to bring students to these basic understandings.

Chapter 4

The Four Plots

The content of each story we read in a book or watch on a screen may be different: the possible combinations of characters and incidents are infinite. What is limited is the number of ways in which stories may be told. Northrop Frye has described four basic story forms or plots that remain constant as the constructive principles used to shape story content; his description is the referent for this chapter.

The four "stories" or plots form a ring or circle of stories (see figure 4.2). They merge into one another at their limits. Where they overlap we have romantic comedies, for instance, or ironic tragedies. Within each basic plot are variations of it.

The framework is exemplified in the basic story of the quest of the hero. The circle of stories starts with romance, which develops out of the mythical story of the hero's adventures. His sufferings and trials, his brushes with death, are the focal points of tragedy and irony-satire. The circle ends with comedy, which develops out of the hero's triumph in his successful quest. Taken together, the four basic stories provide an imaginative shape for each aspect of the human experience. No one story is the whole story. All of the stories together are part of the one story: man's quest for his human identity.

The First Story: Romance

The romance story is one of the great narrative patterns devised by the imagination, a form in which wishes come true, goodness always triumphs over evil, where heroes and heroines

FIGURE 4.2.   The Circle of Stories

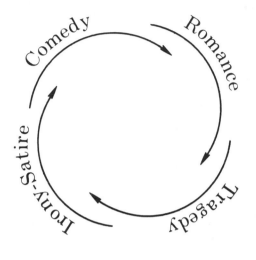

"live happily ever after" in peace and plenty. Although there are variations within the romance form, the basic quest is a cyclical pattern involving three principal stages: a dangerous or marvelous journey; a central struggle, test, or ordeal; and a return to the point from which the journey began. This complete form is most clearly seen in the stories of the epic heroes: Perseus, Theseus, Sigurd, Beowulf, Odysseus.

Other stories, actually episodes within the romance form, may tell of the birth of the hero and his early days. His birth, like that of Moses, is often shrouded in mystery and secrecy. His early life yields stories of extraordinary powers: Paul Bunyan wields his axe in babyhood, Hercules is still an infant when he strangles the serpents sent by Hera to kill him. There may be false "fathers" or "mothers" who seek the child's death; Pharaoh, Herod, and the wicked stepmothers of folk tales are examples. Often the child is prepared for the illustrious life he will lead by kindly foster parents or wise teachers like Merlin in the story of King Arthur.

There are stories of innocence pressing toward experience; an example is Joseph Krumgold's . . . and now Miguel. In other romance stories, the power of innocence overcomes evil or ugliness, as in "Beauty and the Beast" or "Soldier Jack."

Since romance is a wish-fulfillment dream it may also, in some of its forms, show the shadow side of romance: the world we most want to avoid. Here fantasy descends to horror, the hero doing battle with horrible monsters and giants, perhaps even with Death himself. Romance literature in its demonic vein contains the sinister and horrible images associated with nightmares. There are tales of the supernatural, or of magic powers that operate on the side of evil. Frankenstein's creation is like the scary giants and ogres of fairy tales, a dream turned into a nightmare.

On its simplest level the quest is a search for adventure. But, because of its association with the good and the ideal, the quest always has a deeper significance. It is more than adventure for its own sake. The object of the quest determines the seriousness of the tone. Beowulf goes to slay a monster who is laying waste a kingdom; Theseus, to kill the minotaur and put an end to tyranny; Perseus, to destroy the Gorgon Medusa whose terrifying visage turns all who look upon her to stone. Countless sons in folktales go off to seek their fortunes. The quester may be rewarded with something tangible: a treasure, a bride, lands, or a kingdom. He may gain wisdom or magic powers. Symbolically the quest means more. It represents a journey into the darker parts of human nature where the hero confronts evil and even death itself in his efforts to discover his relationship to nature, to other men, to his own self. Whatever tangible treasures may result from the quest, perhaps the greatest benefit is the hero's discovery of himself and his powers. In its deepest sense it seems to be a search for the knowledge of what it means to be human, of what is involved in taking one's place in the pattern of human civilization as a fully functioning member of society.

The hero's quest may be compared to the rites of passage rituals of primitive tribes. Typically the initiate is isolated from his people, given instruction, and made to undergo some ordeal to test his strength or wit. When he has survived the ordeal he is reunited with the tribe amid feasting and rejoicing. He may be given a new name to symbolize his rebirth as a mature member of the society.

The myth of the hero is common to all civilizations, from the ancient Babylonians to contemporary primitive tribes. Its ubiquity suggests that the pattern of romance—the quest—embodies a fundamental pattern of human experience. It has an essential function in the development of the individual's awareness of his strengths and weaknesses, with psychological as well as ritual or tribal significance.

The two central characters of the romance are the hero who is symbolically associated with spring, dawn, youth, and vigor and his adversary who is associated with winter, darkness, old age, and sterility. The hero of romance is often described as being larger-than-life. He is larger not so much because he is superhuman (though he may possess extraordinary powers) but rather in the sense that he has a vision of a world that is more perfect than the one we live in and a belief in his ability to make that world a reality.

The romance hero is a highly idealized figure, usually embodying the virtues held noblest by the societies from which his stories came. He is strong and courteous, durable and self-controlled. He embodies highly civilized virtues like intelligence, wit, and above all, imagination and vision. Although he may not be a god or even the son of one, he has a mysterious contact with a world beyond the world of experience from which he seems to derive a power denied to ordinary mortals. He is a leader, someone at the frontiers of experience. His triumphs benefit all around, his powers lift others toward the heights he scales.

Typical romances move toward progress or fulfillment: victory, the acquisition of treasure, a better life. The achievement involves herculean efforts on the part of the hero, with or without help from others. In the end his life is transformed: he may be released from a threatening past, come to know himself, or be brought to some significant understanding. Most other characters in the romance are one-dimensional. They are either good or bad, for the hero or against him. Good women in romance are usually rescued maidens or brides or supporters of the hero; bad women are cast as evil stepmothers, witches, and temptresses. The people who inhabit the pages of romance are not particularly realistic. They are more like the desirable characters of our dreams and the undesirable characters of our nightmares.

The settings of romance are generally idyllic or at least removed from the world of ordinary experience. There are possibilities of magic and miracles. Things of nature, trees and animals, often have a mysterious rapport with the hero, coming to his aid. Birds warn Snow White of her danger; folk and fairy tales are full of talking animals who aid the hero. We find this in "The Flea," a Spanish folktale, and in the story of "Drakestail."

Visions and revelations are common to romance. In stories that deal with moral opposites it is not surprising that there be some means of connecting a "heavenly" world with a "lower" one. The union is frequently achieved by a vision or insight (in more modern romances) that takes place in a high or isolated place like a mountaintop, an island, or a tower. Jacob's ladder is an example of this enjoinment of the two worlds.

The Tale of Peter Rabbit, durable and delightful, has been a source of literary satisfaction to generations of youngsters. It is a prime example of the well-constructed story, an example of the romance form in miniature. The hero faces a perilous journey with minor adventures, a crucial struggle, and final exaltation or success, the whole expressing the passage from a point of ritual death to the "resurrection" of the recognition scene.

Peter sets out in defiance of his mother to seek identity, an identity undoubtedly associated with his father who had met an untimely death in Mr. McGregor's garden. The young adventurer undergoes a series of hairsbreadth escapes. He loses his jacket and shoes, is wet and frightened, and escapes only after he finds himself a vantage point that gives him, together with his fleetness of foot, an advantage over his enemy. In the end, as a result of his own efforts, he is safely home, undoubtedly a proven hero, although he has lost his clothes, is not feeling well, and is put to bed with a dose of camomile tea. His well-behaved siblings have bread and milk and blackberries for supper, but it is Peter who is most emphatically the hero of the piece since he is the one who has successfully completed a quest.

The characterization in *Peter Rabbit* follows the typical conflict pattern of the romance. There are two main characters: Peter, the protagonist, and Mr. McGregor, the antagonist. At the lowest point of his trials, when he is imprisoned in the gooseberry net, Peter is encouraged by three friendly sparrows who "implored him to exert himself," characters with literary relatives among the children-of-nature figures common to romance, morally neutral and helpful to the hero. The very proper siblings are foils for Peter, emphasizing by their docility the enormity of Peter's ambition and daring. The comforting figure of Mrs. Rabbit waiting at home until the hero finishes his wanderings is similar to wife-mother figures in more ambitious and lengthier works: Solveig of *Peer Gynt*, for example, and Penelope in the *Odyssey*.

For older children, *Call It Courage* is another example of the romance plot. Mafatu, son of the great chief of a Polynesian tribe, lives in fear of the sea, for as a young child he came perilously close to drowning, while his mother lost her life as she rescued him. He is reduced to women's work on the island, scorned by his peers as a coward, and a disappointment to his father. The reason for Mafatu's quest is clear—he must find his identity in a face-to-face battle with his enemy, the sea.

Mafatu sets out on his perilous journey, weathering a storm and the destruction of his canoe on a reef. Finally he reaches a desolate island where he sets to work to make a shelter and replacements for the canoe and the weapons he has lost. The sheltering island itself contains a threat, for it is the site of the holy place of sacrifice of a cannibal tribe who will surely return and seek to destroy Mafatu when they know he has desecrated their sacred ground. Yet he sets out calmly to build his boat, gaining courage with every action of his own hand. He kills a wild boar with a weapon of his own making, saves his dog from a tiger shark, and kills an octopus in a daring underwater fight. Drums announce the arrival of the cannibals, but Mafatu's boat is ready and he eludes his pursuers with skill and daring, and sails in the direction of home. He cries out triumphantly to the threatening sea that he no longer fears it, even when there seems little chance of his reaching home again. Mafatu at this moment has won his personal battle and regained his identity. It remains, however, for him to be exalted in the eyes of others and this happens when he lands safely home, a figure of mystery and magnificence.

In *Call It Courage* the sea is the antagonist, a personification of a being of unlimited strength, bent for revenge. Mafatu's only friends are misfits like himself: a nondescript yellow dog and a lame albatross. Like neutral nature spirits, they play a helping role: comforting the boy, giving him hope and companionship. And, in the case of Kivi the albatross, offering mysterious guidance as Mafatu begins his quest and ends it.

The romance form is popular in children's literature. It is found in picture storybooks like Maurice Sendak's *Where the Wild Things Are*, Edward Ardizzone's *Little Tim and the Brave Sea Captain*, Hardie Gramatky's *Little Toot*. The hero tales retold in language suitable for modern eyes and ears, particularly those written recently by Ian Serraillier and Roger Lancelyn Green, are superb examples of this form. William Steig's *Dominic* is, in structure, another fine specimen of the romance form.

Although it may appear with widely different subject matter and expressing a variety of values, the romance plot or pattern has always been a favorite with children and those who write for them. Whether the romance is close to myth and magic like the old tales of heroes, a fantasy, or a realistic modern version of the form, there is no question about its power and importance in the development of the imagination. Romance tells of dreams and how they are made to come true. It deals in hope. It brings a message from the imagination to the imagination that every child will need if he is to slay his dragons.

The Second Story: Tragedy

Romance, as a story form, tells of wishes and dreams that come true. Poems and stories that explore the *limits* of man's power to make his wishes and dreams come true belong to the literary form we call tragedy. Destruction of the innocent, beautiful, or virtuous is something we feel should not happen. Yet such destruction is a fact of the human experience, no matter how unreasonable it may seem to us. Tragedy leaves us feeling helpless and vulnerable and reminds us that we are not all-powerful. Tragic stories often suggest that the hero is destroyed because he has broken some natural law or order, even though he may have done so in all innocence. They are imaginative attempts to balance man's potential greatness with his perishable nature, to come to terms with powers that are greater than his.

The central idea of tragedy is catastrophe or death befalling a heroic character. A tragedy may be romantic or ironic and realistic, depending on whether it features idealized or more realistic heroes and heroines. At the heroic extreme the tragic hero is given the greatest possible dignity, usually a product of his innocence and courage. Hans Christian Andersen's "Steadfast Tin Soldier" is such a hero, Balder of Norse mythology is another.

Another kind of heroic tragedy is the archetypal story of the loss of innocence, innocence being a lack of experience. Young people are baffled and defeated by their first contact with the adult world, as is Jane in Helen Fern Daringer's *Adopted Jane*. Such stories may tell of a youthful life cut off or of a child's first understanding of the significance of death.

Still another variation of the tragic story tells of the death, often a willing one, of the hero in support of some great cause. Beowulf deliberately gives his life to save his people. King Arthur knows that his whole life has been a sacrifice for a "dream of justice." This type of tragic story derives from the ancient ritual of the scapegoat: the evils of the tribe were ritualistically invested in an animal who was then driven into the wilderness to die. In the tragedy of sacrifice, the hero's society is purged of evil by his sacrifice, voluntarily made in their behalf.

The tragedy of sacrifice is a grave reminder of what it costs to be fully human in the noblest sense. The hero accepts fate and resists oppression at the cost of his life, his sacrifice saves those left behind. It is a sobering story but an exhilarating one, found in both epic tales like Beowulf and biographies of such men as Martin Luther King and Malcolm X.

Many tragic stories center around a character who is not of the world of innocence but of the world of experience. He is a puzzling character; he may be a great leader of men and in many respects heroic, but at the same time his character or outlook contains a flaw that leads him to make some disastrous mistake or choice. His action seems to provoke a situation that causes his inevitable downfall, a sense of his having disturbed the natural order. His story seems a kind of revenge, a hostile reaction from some power that is beyond him. Great classical tragedies like *Antigone* and *King Lear* are stories of this type.

As tragedy gets closer to irony in the circle of stories, heroes become more lifelike, no longer the larger-than-life figures just spoken of. Here are stories that reflect man's feeling of being caught in a trap from which he cannot free himself, of being a victim of vast and overwhelming forces that immobilize and imprison. In ironic literature we see man's spirit defeated under similar conditions. But in tragedy, even when all hope is lost, man retains his human dignity. By the very act of facing the realities and challenges of life, he overcomes them.

William Armstrong's *Sounder* shows us elements of this last type of tragic story. The father is a victim of circumstances beyond his control, a black sharecropper in Louisiana during the Depression. His opportunities are limited. Both nature and men are hostile. The land bears poor crops, and no one comes forward to help him feed his starving children; when he steals for them, his captors are ruthless in their punishment. Yet he endures through agonies of pain when the posse's guns injure him and through the knowledge of his family's suffering when he is taken off to prison. He returns home, body broken but spirit intact, to die with dignity, leaving that and his courage as a legacy of hope to his children.

Many children's stories have elements of tragedy in them but few are examples of the tragic form as we find it in adult literature. *Pigeon, Fly Home*, a tragic story that deals with the destruction of a brave innocent, is no less tragic because the victim is a pigeon rather than a human being. Chad and his friends have a pigeon racing club, and he takes pity on the coffee-colored peeper that is the weakling of his flock. He tries to shelter it from the stronger pigeons who threaten to peck it to death, nurturing it against the advice of his fellow pigeon-fanciers who are able to view with more professional detachment the fate of weakling peepers.

Yet Chad is determined that his Leyden will not share the fate of the weak bird among the strong. He feeds her, protects her, and insulates himself from the jibes of less compassionate breeders.

Eventually his pigeon comes into her own and is accepted by the flock.

Then, on her first flight, Leyden is attacked by a hawk. She returns home, safe but injured and unsteady, and is once again almost pecked to death by the others. Still Chad persists, though his efforts amount to perversity in the eyes of his less sentimental friends.

At last it seems that Chad's stubborn faith has been rewarded when Leyden becomes the best racer in the flock. Her early difficulties seem all in the past and Chad's hopes are high as he enters her in the big race of the season. She would have won, but at the height of her triumph she is attacked and brought down by two hawks. Hunters see her last gallant struggle and report how bravely she died.

Leyden's ability and final courage have won the admiration of the club members who once doubted her, and all of them share Chad's sense of helplessness and loss. But no one has words adequate to explain why Leyden's life was marked with tragedy.

The tragic story leaves us with a sense of wonder and awe. It raises questions men have never found answers for, fundamental questions about the ills that living creatures are subject to. Tragedy, as opposed to irony, does not leave us with a sense of hopelessness. The tragic figure may suffer, even die, but he characteristically displays the highest of human attributes: nobility and dignity.

The Third Story: Satire and Irony

Satire and irony are literary forms set in the world of experience, reflecting the discrepancy between what is and what ideally ought to be. Satire attempts to change man and society for the better, often by using bitter ridicule; irony details human limitations.

Both forms often parody the themes and archetypes of romance to make their points. The hero is not larger-than-life; he is all-too-human. He is subject to all the ills of the world: physical weakness, other man's inhumanity, his own neuroses. Time passes and he must grow old and die. There is no feeling, as there is in tragedy and romance, of mysterious powers that link the hero to something that transcends the world. Since he is merely man in a world that is far from ideal, his quests often remain unfulfilled or they are wrong-headed or without goals. The qualities of the hero—clear vision, endurance, ability—are absent. Or they are used by the hero-as-rogue who outwits the unscrupulous by becoming unscrupulous himself. The good and innocent are more likely to be victims than champions, and love is more often thwarted than conquering. The green world of romance is often replaced by the harsh concrete of the city slum.

In a sense the satirist is himself like the questing hero of romance. He chips away at the huge ills of humanity: hypocrisy, self-deceit, smugness, pettiness, injustice, but with little hope of curing them. In some satires people are shown accepting what they believe cannot be changed or retreating into rationalizations in an effort to escape it. There are stories granting that the world is full of crime and folly but counseling the reader to keep his balance, remember the tried and true, laugh at the follies around him and, in effect, accept the conventions of society.

Most satire is beyond the imaginative reach of young children, and few authors write in this form for them. The satirical aspects of *Gulliver's Travels* and *Alice in Wonderland* are for the most part absorbed without notice as the story is enjoyed for its own sake. In Andersen's tales such as "The Ugly Duckling" and "The Emperor's New Clothes" children encounter the satire in a form more manageable by them. *Elements* of satire occur, however, in contemporary children's fiction like *Henry 3, Freaky Friday, The Shrinking of Treehorn, Konrad,* and *The Pushcart War.* Like irony, satire in books for children is often softened through fantasy and humor. Both *Konrad* and *The Pushcart War* are excellent examples. *Konrad* is a thoroughly delightful spoof on the wonders of a technological society that produces everything, even babies made to order in test tubes. The highly original *Pushcart War* features a brave army of pushcart owners who outwit big business in New York City.

Ironic stories, like satiric ones, take place in the world of experience rather than in the world of innocence and with them, too, heroism is impossible. They differ from satire in that no moral ideal seems possible.

In recent years more and more children's literature has been written in the ironic mode of most contemporary adult literature. *The Pigman* by Paul Zindel, a story written for young adolescents, looks at tragedy from below, from the moral and realistic perspective of the state of experience. It stresses the humanity of its heroes, minimizes the sense of ritual inevitability found in tragedy, and supplies social and psychological explanations for catastrophe.

In *The Pigman* two precocious, perceptive, and lonely teenagers make friends with an equally lonely, strange old man, Mr. Pignati, who lives only through dreams of his dead wife and daily visits to his closest friend, a baboon at the zoo. The story is narrated alternately by the hero and heroine in a series of flashbacks, their attempt to make sense of all the crazy things they did. It is often funny in its digressions, wit, and candor, but the humor only serves to point up the irony that underlies it.

Alienated from their parents, John and Lorraine find the Pigman someone who accepts them as they are, spoils them a little, and genuinely enjoys their company, luxuries not to be found in their homes. Their zany relationship flourishes in love and laughter; they have the run of his cluttered old house, sharing with him food and trips to the zoo. He buys them gifts of roller skates and all three joyously skate down the hallway of his home. Human weakness and poor judgment are their undoing. Mr. Pignati suffers a heart attack after an hilarious skating session. While he is hospitalized, John and Lorraine invite friends to a party that turns his house into a shambles. His wife's collection of prized china pigs is smashed, her clothes ripped by the girls who dress up in them, and his belongings looted. In the midst of the chaos Mr. Pignati returns from the hospital. Although he forgives the stricken young people who are not sure how things got so far out of their control, his gay spirit is broken. When they persuade him the next day to take a trip to the zoo to see Bobo, his baboon friend, he agrees half-heartedly to go. Once there he discovers that Bobo has died while he was in the hospital. Mr. Pignati, weak from the heart attack, dies in front of the baboon cage.

John tries to sum up his feelings at the end, deploring life "in a world where you can grow old and be alone and have to get down on your hands and knees and beg for friends." He muses that maybe he and Lorraine for that matter are baboons, only of a different kind, and that his parents and everyone else are "baffled baboons concentrating on all the wrong things." The young people have faced reality and themselves, and found both confrontations unpleasant.

As structure, the central principle of ironic myth is best approached as a parody of romance. Simple though it is, "The Gingerbread Boy" is a good primer introduction to the ironic myth. The Gingerbread Boy, about to be eaten, escapes and rolls down the hill on a quest for freedom and safety, narrowly escaping all who would eat him, and that is everyone he meets, including the family from whom he first escaped. Freedom seems certain until the Gingerbread Boy makes a friend of Piggy Wiggy, who proves false. In the process of what seems a helpful act of carrying the Gingerbread Boy across a brook on his snout, the pig swallows him in one gulp. The Gingerbread Boy's quest is cut short unfulfilled.

Other stories in the ironic mode include John Neufeld's *Edgar Allen*, Eleanor Estes's *The Hundred Dresses*, Mary Weik's *The Jazz Man*, Robert Burch's *Queenie Peavy*, Helen Fern Daringer's *Adopted Jane*, Marilyn Sach's *The Bears' House*, John Donovan's *Wild in the World*, Louise Fitzhugh's *Nobody's Family's Going to Change*, and M. E. Kerr's *Dinky Hocker Shoots Smack*. The novels by Fitzhugh and Kerr illustrate how humor is used to ease the pain of irony in stories for young people.

The ironic mode is further accommodated in children's stories that use toys, animals, and diminutive people as protagonists. In this mode the protagonist is inferior in power even to ordinary people, a victim of others and the powers of nature and inferior in power and intelligence to the reader, who has the sense of looking down on a scene of entrapment, frustration, and absurdity.

However, the animal, toy, or diminutive characters do not necessarily see *themselves* as ironic victims. Rather, like William Steig's Dominic, they may see themselves as protagonists in the adventurous world of romance in which danger is great but where honorable motives, courage, and determination are rewarded. Excellent examples of such protagonists are found in *The Borrowers* and its several sequels, written by Mary Norton.

By using animals, toys, or diminutive characters as protagonists, authors are able to present an ironic view of life while at the same time preserving the optimism and positive values of the comic and romantic modes, traditionally considered the most appropriate for children's literature.

Ironic stories reveal a bitter picture of human existence: the contrast between ideals and reality. Today many people believe that children's literature must reflect life as it is and not see it through the rose-colored glasses of romance and comedy. There is merit in this view, of course, but irony and satire do not present the whole story of man's experience any more than romance and comedy do. Irony, in fact, proves to be romance turned upside down, the nightmare instead of the dream. That they are the two sides of one coin is proof that we need them both. Implicit in the ironic story is the dream of how things "ought to be."

The Fourth Story: Comedy

When we speak of comedy, we are likely to think of laughter, but many forms of the comic plot in literature are not necessarily funny or humorous. They do, however, present a positive view of the human experience. Comedy is a form that celebrates the power of nature, human or otherwise, to renew itself, the power of life to overthrow the threat of death. It has to do with transformation, with the power of the imagination to raise experience above the limits of time and space, to change people and things into desirable images.

The central idea of comedy is rebirth or renewal after obstacles are overcome. The simplest pattern of comedy is expressed in the old cliché: boy meets girl, boy loses girl, boy and girl are reunited. The hero is kept from the object of his desires by a series of blocks or obstacles, often in the form of the intransigent adult. The comic form usually involves a movement from one kind of society to another: from the rule of impossible, unreasonable people to the establishment of a new society where everyone is happy.

This ending is achieved by almost any means at all: miraculous transformations, coincidences, magical interventions. But the audience is delighted even when the solution is most improbable, because they know that this is the only possible ending, that this is the way things ought to be. Even the intransigent characters are reformed and redeemed and become part of the new social order in the end. Scrooge in Dickens's *A Christmas Carol* is one of these.

The typical hero of comedy is like Wilbur in E. B. White's *Charlotte's Web*: likeable enough, but rather ordinary and conventional. He is aided by a cunning cohort, Charlotte, a character type common to comedy, one related to the "tricky slave" of ancient Roman comedies whose wit and daring frequently saved his charming but none-too-bright master. The chief blocking character is often a father figure, an outright villain, or is represented by an unfair or impossible situation that must be overcome, like the threat to Wilbur's life. Other comic characters include detractors of the hero, like Templeton the rat, and buffoons who contribute to the comic action with singing, clowning, and miscellaneous humor, like the gossipy goose in *Charlotte's Web*.

Like tragedies, comic plots may stretch from the limits of the ironic to the romantic. Julia Cunningham's *Dorp Dead* is an ironic comedy where the will to live triumphs over odds that must surely have left scars. *Charlotte's Web* and White's *The Trumpet of the Swan* are romantic comedies at the other end of the scale; from beginning to end the mood is one of hope.

An excellent example of the comic structure in children's literature is *The 500 Hats of Bartholomew Cubbins*, a comedy in the phase closest to romance. In this story there is a magical element that is never explained: the five hundred hats that appear successively on Bartholomew's head are a phenomenon that "just 'happened to happen' and was not very likely to happen again."

Bartholomew, much like the heroes of Dickensian comedy, is a likeable chap, unpretentious and brave enough when he must be. Through no fault of his own, he is confronted with a wrathful and unreasonable king who demands that Bartholomew remove his hat in his presence. The hero tries to comply but cannot—whenever he removes a hat, another appears in its place. Like the hero of a picaresque tale, a juvenile Tom Jones, he is whirled off into a series of adventures, more or less an innocent victim of circumstances and situations largely beyond his control.

The characters are typical figures of comedy. The king is a blustering and unreasonable figure, foolish in his repeated attempts to divest Bartholomew of his offending hats. His retinue includes buffoon types reminiscent of the cooks and clowns of Shakespeare: the pompous prime minister, the ineffective and humorous wise men and magicians.

Bartholomew faces death bravely and calmly enough in his stolid way until he is saved, and in the nick of time, by the magic powers that brought him into danger in the first place. The final hats grow more and more magnificent until the vain and greedy king, behaving true to character, covets one for his own. He pays Bartholomew a substantial sum for the splendid five hundredth, places it over his crown, and is appeased at last. Arm-in-arm he and Bartholomew gaze out over the royal domain from the same vantage point, as equals. How such a reversal is accomplished is inherent in the comic structure itself. Everything moves toward the "happy ending" with the blocking characters converted to the hero's side.

The old tale of Cinderella is a prime example of the comic structure, its pattern enduring in displacements old and new and yet to come. It exemplifies comedy in the phase closest to romance for it involves magical manifestations and metamorphoses. Cinderella endures against the impossible odds of a cruel and unreasonable stepmother and her daughters who thwart her every wish and desire, including preventing her attendance at the prince's ball. Then her goodness is rewarded, the fairy godmother transforms her utterly. She must do as she is told (and she is used to that) and all will be well.

Cinderella at last is received into the society in which we all knew from the beginning she belonged; it is in effect a movement from illusion to reality. The illusion is always negative forces that must be dispelled, caused as they are by hypocrisy, disguise, and the like. Cinderella, of course, was really a princess in disguise, although it did not seem so at first. But the reader knows this, the prince recognizes it, and the king and queen receive her at the end as if she were a long-lost daughter. The character of Cinderella is the embodiment of a wish-fullment: virtue and goodness are rewarded; things turn out "as they should."

The comic form is a favorite of writers for children, found in countless traditional tales like "Beauty and the Beast" and "Snow White and the Seven Dwarfs," and in modern novels like Doris Gates's *Blue Willow* and Anne Holm's *North to Freedom.*

The main emphasis in comic literature, then, is on the creation of a new order. This is often achieved by equating the new and better world with the season of spring, a time of beginnings and renewal. The world at the end of a typical comedy is a new one, better and more ordered, freer and more merciful than the old order it replaced. The marriage and the happy ending typical of comedies is symbolic of the establishment of a new, more just society. The biblical Book of Revelation uses the marriage metaphor to symbolize an eventual happy ending to the story of mankind. A bride from earth, known variously as the New Jerusalem, the church, or the community of saints, is united with the redeemer and with him enters paradise. The central form of the comic story is symbolic of hope, of possibilities for new and renewed life, of the power of love.

To sum up: the main idea of romance, the first story, is adventure or action. An innocent, idealized person moves in a world beyond the ordinary and realistic world of experience and undergoes a quest involving a test of his human powers. The central idea of tragedy, the second story, is catastrophe or death befalling a hero who maintains those qualities humans consider heroic no matter what his fate. Tragedies may be romantic or ironic depending on whether they feature idealized characters or more realistic ones. The controlling idea of satire and irony is the absence of heroism and the presence of chaos, confusion, misery, and injustice—the world of experience. Satire attempts to change the unsatisfactory condition by revealing such things as hypocrisy through ridicule. The ironist simply shows things as he sees them and his point of view is a negative one. Comedy, the fourth story, moves out of ironic confusion with its central idea the human spirit's potential for renewal.

It ends with a transformation of ironic chaos. The comic spirit is one of hope for the future and faith in human endurance over time.

The stories that man tells are parts of a single story. That one story is mankind's search for his human identity, a search that continues and will continue as long as there are people. It begins with an ideal world, moves through the less perfect world of human experience, and toward an ideal time when the perfection of the lost Eden is returned to us. This is the restoration promised in Revelation 21:4.

> And God shall wipe away all tears from their eyes; and there shall be no more death, neither sorrow, nor crying, neither shall there be any more pain: for the former things are passed away.

Literature, of course, is not religion. It does not address itself to belief. What it does provide is an imaginative vision. There are moments when we catch a glimpse of that perfect world. For it exists in the mind of the imaginative writer and in imaginations awakened by his words.

A knowledge of the structural principles of literature is reserved for the teacher. It should be obvious that this abstract framework is not something to be imposed upon the child as a piece of memory work. It is the teacher's business to know it and to structure the student's experiences with literature in such a way that the child will discover for himself the significant patterns in literature at the same time as he enjoys each literary experience for its own sake. The good teacher is one who can help students see significant patterns in facts. A teacher of literature has dual goals: that students will experience poems and stories with pleasure, and that they will grow in their knowledge of literature as a whole. The impact of literature upon the imagination is that much greater where there is an awareness of its unity.

Chapter 5

Theory into Practice

Our educational system may be compared to a pyramid. The elementary curriculum is the broad base on which the whole of the enormous structure rests and should provide adequate structural support for what is built upon it.

In recent years there has been a growing tendency to upgrade elementary education, to recognize that the younger student is capable of significant intellectual achievement. University scholars have increasingly participated in planning curricula for their disciplines that extend from kindergarten to graduate school, particularly in the areas of science and mathematics. From the famous Woods Hole Conference of 1959 came a key word that has dominated educational theory ever since. That key word is "structure."

Elementary education need not be intellectually insignificant, for once the structure of a discipline is understood *by the teacher*, it can be presented to the child in ways that are appropriate to his level of development. If the foundation of early learning is sound, later learning may be accomplished with greater ease and precision.

Basic Principles of Literary Criticism

Until now the study of literature has lacked a comprehensive theory that reveals its inherent structure. Many have believed that literature, because it is art and not science, cannot be considered structurally. Northrop Frye's theory provides proof that it can. Once the structural principles of literature are established, the teaching of literature, or criticism, can follow a deductive pattern, be considerably simplified and clarified, and proceed progressively and systematically.

Frye's conceptual framework provides a needed added dimension to literary studies. It allows us to see the shape of literature *as a whole,* defining and placing its separate parts much as a globe defines and places each of the land and water masses of the earth. The framework produces a means of unifying and integrating discrete literary experiences; within it, each experience may be examined *as an entity* and also recognized as part of the total form of literature. The fundamental principles of Frye's scheme may be summarized as follows:

—The literary imagination seeks to associate and identify the human mind with what goes on outside of it. The language of literature is associative, using figures of speech such as simile and metaphor to suggest this identity. In the *imaginative* logic of literary thought and language, therefore, two quite unlike things may be said to be like each other or to be each other. ("My love is like a rose"; "My love *is* a rose.")

Freed from the boundaries set by reason and logic, the human imagination is unlimited, constructing possible models of human experience. These models or constructs illustrate the extent of imagination: In the world of the imagination there are no limits; anything goes that is imaginatively possible.

We participate in literary experiences primarily through the imagination, not the reason, which means that we often must suspend disbelief as we accept the premises of poem or story. Literature educates the imagination by illustrating its own unlimited range and by extending our personal visions of possibilities. For young children, experience with fantasy and selected lyric poetry serves particularly well to illustrate imaginative logic while it stretches the imagination.

—Literature begins with and develops out of mythology, where the process of identification began with primitive people's efforts to identify themselves imaginatively with animals, plants, and the forces of nature. Their identity with these objects and energies appeared to them to be necessary for survival, or at least for emotional security in a hostile world. With identity ("I am the eagle," "My mother is a sea nymph") came control—imaginative control over nature.

As civilization advanced, people concerned themselves more with human problems and conflicts than with their relationship to non–human nature. The gods and heroes of myth and legend gave way to stories about ordinary people and moved toward realism. However, no mater how "realistic" stories become, an examination of figures of speech, images, and symbols shows that people still strive to come to terms, through story and poetry, with alien nature. (For examples of this in contemporary children's literature, see Julia Cunningham's *Come to the Edge* and Armstrong Sperry's *Call It Courage*.)

—In transforming "nature" into an imaginative world, the imagination seized on the element of regular repetition in nature, its cyclical rhythms: the four seasons, day and night, the water cycle. These natural cycles became identified with the cycle of human life. Myths, the first literature, feature many stories of gods or heroes who undergo successful adventures, die or disappear, and are eventually reborn. (Perseus, Theseus, Orpheus, and Hercules are examples.) Out of this cycle of death and renewal, there gradually emerged four fundamental types of imaginative experience, a "circle of stories," which relate to the triumph, death, or disappearance of a god or hero and his rebirth: romance, tragedy, irony, comedy.

—Literature has a dialectical as well as a cyclical understructure. The imagination projects two limits: what we hate and fear (hell) opposed to what we love and desire (heaven). These constructs appear in literature as the idealized world of romance and the frustrated, suffering world of irony-satire.

—The cyclical and dialectical structures underlie all literary imagery, forming a framework within which all literary works, individually and together, represent people's imaginative efforts to recapture a sense of identity with their surroundings. This quest for identity is the "one story" of literature.

The quester's story connects the two opposite limits of the human imagination: the quester is someone with whom we want to identify; his enemies and negative experiences are what we want to avoid. The story character's quest is an effort to regain identity, to restore the harmony and perfection of the lost paradise or golden age of the human imagination. "Identity" of course refers not only to discovering one's name or paternity (though this is often the case on the surface of many stories) but also to the reestablishing of a lost unity or oneness with nature or some social group.

Through the language of identification—simile and metaphor—imaginative writers try to lead us back, through our imaginations, to our lost identity. We recognize ourselves in the characters they create; we realize that they often express thoughts we feel but have no words to express. This story of the loss and regaining of identity is the framework of all literature. As William Blake said: "The nature of my work is visionary and imaginative; it is an attempt to restore what the ancients called the Golden Age."

—Fictional literature, as we have noted earlier, begins with myth and proceeds along a chronological continuum in a series of displacements toward "realism." As the displacement progresses, the powers of the protagonist are diminished. In myth we have godlike heroes with magical powers; in contemporary ironic realism we have powerless figures who are helpless victims of themselves or others.

—Since literature grows out of the literature that came before it, it derives its forms from itself and is therefore conventional. What writers read provides them with conventions, typical and socially accepted ways of writing. Certain conventions are common to certain types of stories or poems, no matter how far these are separated in time. For example, there are conventional plots and characters: The Cinderella "story" keeps recurring even in today's television commercials, where, like the fairy godmother, a mouthwash transforms the social failure into a success. The hero whose birth is shrouded in mystery is a convention as old as the story of Moses and as new as that of Superman.

Archetypes (certain *recurring* conventions, images, symbols, characters, and narrative patterns) are the concepts that give literature its unity. These archetypes include an archetypal story, the quest myth, that informs all narrative literature.

—In literary imagery certain seasons of the year and times of day are characteristically related to happiness, youth, and beginnings while others are related to sorrow, old age, and endings. Certain colors and natural settings are used recurrently to reflect particular moods and atmospheres. The two dreams of humans are expressed symbolically in literature: at one limit is the wasteland or wilderness; at the other is a vision of a garden or paradise. Certain animals, birds, and natural phenomena are associated positively with human hopes, dreams, and desires and others negatively with what people reject as undesirable.

—A work of literature moves in time, like music, but it has also a *structure* and may be studied all in one piece after it is experienced. It also has a context within literature; it is more like certain works than like others. Knowledge of literature grows through identifying likenesses in what is read or listened to.

—Knowledge of literature grows through noting likenesses in literary *and* sub-literary experience: comics, television, advertising, conversation. (The Jack-the-giant-killer story is like the biblical story of David and Goliath, the television commercial in which a tiny pill defeats a giant headache, and the Tom and Jerry cartoon that shows a little mouse getting the better of a large cat.)

—Works of literature are constructs made of words, and the myths and images of literature recur in and give form to *all* structures built of words. Experience and knowledge of literature helps us to evaluate *all* of our verbal experience. We recognize progress myths in the speeches of politicians, for instance, and pastoral myths in advertisements in which products are used by happy, youthful people by a stream in a wooded grove.

These basic understandings concerning the structure of literature provide a deductive framework *for the teacher* to use as a guide in the process of communicating to students that literature is not merely a collection of separate works but *an order of words,* related like members of a large family, with a family tree traceable to the earliest times. The student is led toward these understandings inductively. With the deductive framework provided by the literary principles as a guide, the teacher structures *learning sequences* that begin with *experiencing* of literature and continue with *response* to it. Some suggestions about structuring learning sequences follow. (Specific examples of learning sequences are found in Chapters 6 and 7.)

Structuring Learning Sequences
in Literary Criticism

A *learning sequence* in literary criticism may be a single session or a series of sessions, depending upon its purpose. It involves two aspects of the critical process: experiencing literature and responding to it. Response may take many forms. In classrooms it usually begins with discussion, but other responses are as legitimate in the critical process. Writing, dramatizing, drawing, and sculpting are examples. The extent and type of response depend upon the purpose of the sequence. Questioning and discussion need not follow every listening or independent reading activity. Through oral reading and subsequent discussion of an experience-in-common, as described later in this chapter, students may be prepared to make personal and private responses to books they read independently. Often, if questions do follow the experiencing of a poem or story, they should be the children's own. Responses need to be varied, with opportunity provided for nonverbal forms such as a dramatization in pantomime, a drawing, or a clay model.

In the elementary and middle school, listening to literature is of primary importance in the critical process. Besides the pleasure of hearing a good reader interpret a fine poem or story, students, especially those who don't read easily and well, have the opportunity to experience stories and poems as artistic entities. Wide, independent reading—experiencing quantities of literature—is central to the literary study described in this book. For the teacher's guidance, specific suggestions follow for reading aloud to children and for planning independent reading sessions.

Reading Aloud

Material for oral reading is chosen on the basis of its literary excellence and wide appeal. In poetry, most children prefer contemporary poems. They enjoy stories in verse, humor, word play, outrageous comparisons, repetition, strong rhythms, and rhyme. There follows a highly selective list of poetry sources. From them teachers would select poems to suit a particular group or serve a special instructional purpose.

POETRY FOR YOUNGER CHILDREN

Anthologies

Agree, Rose (comp.). *How To Eat a Poem and Other Morsels* with illus. by Peggy Wilson (Pantheon, 1967).
Cole, William (ed.). *Oh, What Nonsense!* with illus. by Tomi Ungerer (Viking, 1966).
Livingston, Myra Cohn (comp.). *Listen, Children, Listen: An Anthology of Poems for the Very Young* with illus. by Trina Schart Hyman (Harcourt, 1972).
Schenk de Regniers, Beatrice, and others (comps.). *Poems Children Will Sit Still For* (Scholastic, 1969).

Individual Poets

Aldis, Dorothy. *All Together: A Child's Treasury of Verse* with illus. by Helen D. Jameson, Marjorie Flack, and Margaret Freeman (Putnam, 1952).

Chute, Marchette. *Rhymes About Us* with illus. by the author (Dutton, 1974).

Fisher, Aileen. *My Cat Has Eyes of Sapphire Blue* with illus. by Marie Anel (Crowell, 1973).

Hoban, Russell. *Egg Thoughts and Other Frances Songs* with illus. by Lillian Hoban (Harper, 1972).

Jacobs, Leland. *Is Somewhere Always Far Away?* with illus. by John E. Johnson (Holt, 1967).

Kuskin, Karla. *Any Me I Want To Be* with illus. by the author (Harper, 1972).

Livingston, Myra Cohn. *I'm Hiding* with illus. by Eril Blegvad (Harcourt, 1961).

McCord, David. *Every Time I Climb a Tree* with illus. by Marc Simont (Little, Brown, 1967).

Merriam, Eve. *It Doesn't Always Have To Rhyme* with illus. by Malcolm Spooner (Atheneum, 1974).

Milne, A. A. *When We Were Very Young,* and *Now We Are Six* with illus. by E. H. Shephard (Dutton, 1924, 1927).

Prelutsky, Jack. *The Queen of Eene* with illus. by Wendy Watson (Greenwillow, 1978).

Worth, Valerie. *Small Poems* with illus. by Natalie Babbitt (Farrar, 1972).

POETRY FOR OLDER CHILDREN

Anthologies

Adoff, Arnold (comp.). *I Am the Darker Brother: An Anthology of Modern Poems by Negro Americans* with illus. by Benny Andrews (Macmillan, 1968).

Arbuthnot, May H., and Root, Shelton L., Jr. (comps.). *Time for Poetry,* 3rd ed. (Scott, Foresman, 1968).

Colum, Padriac (ed.). *Roofs of Gold: Poems to Read Aloud* (Macmillan, 1964).

De La Mare, Walter (comp.). *Come Hither* with illus. by Warren Chappell (Knopf, 1957).

Dunning, Stephen, and others (comps.). *Reflections on a Gift of Watermelon Pickle* (Scott, Foresman, 1966).

Prelutsky, Jack (comp.). *The Random House Book of Poetry for Children* with illus. by Arnold Lobel (Random House, 1983).

Tashjian, Virginia. *With a Deep Sea Smile: Story Hour Stretches for Large and Small Groups* with illus. by Rosemary Wells (Little, Brown, 1974). Also by Tashjian, *Juba This and Juba That* (Little, Brown, 1969). Both are collections of short stories, poems, tongue twisters, finger plays, and jokes.

Untermeyer, Louis (ed.). *The Golden Treasury of Poetry* with illus. by Joan Anglund (Golden Press, 1959).

Individual Poets

Aiken, Joan. *The Skin Spinners* with illus. by Ken Rinciari (Viking, 1976).

Behn, Harry. *The Wizard in the Well* with illus. by the author (Harcourt, 1956).

Ciardi, John. *The Reason for the Pelican* with illus. by Madeleine Gekeire (Lippincott, 1959).

De La Mare, Walter. *Peacock Pie* with illus. by Barbara Cooney (Knopf, 1961).

Farjeon, Eleanor. *Poems for Children* with illus. by Lucinda Wakefield (Lippincott, 1951).

Field, Rachel. *Poems* with illus. by the author (Macmillan, 1957).

Giovanni, Nikki. *Ego Tripping and Other Poems for Young Readers* with illus. by George Ford (Lawrence Hill, 1974).

Hughes, Langston. *Don't You Turn Back: Poems,* selected by Lee Bennett Hopkins, with illus. by Ann Grifalconi (Knopf, 1969).

McCord, David. *One at a Time: His Collected Poems for the Young* (Little, Brown, 1977).

Merriam, Eve. *Out Loud* (Atheneum, 1973).

Nash, Ogden. *The Old Dog Barks Backwards* with illus. by Robert Binks (Little, 1972).

O'Neill, Mary. *Hailstones and Halibut Bones* with illus. by Leonard Weisgard (Doubleday), 1961).

Silverstein, Shel. *Where the Sidewalk Ends* with illus. by the author (Harper, 1974).

———. *A Light in the Attic* (Harper, 1981).

Viorst, Judith. *If I Were in Charge of the World and Other Worries* (Atheneum, 1981).

STORIES FOR YOUNGER CHILDREN

Stories in verse are excellent choices for reading aloud. So are those featuring repetitive patterns and refrains. As an example, here is the refrain that for decades young listeners have enjoyed chanting as they listen to the timeless favorite, *Millions of Cats* by Wanda Gág.

Cats here, cats there,
Cats and kittens everywhere,

Hundreds of cats,
Thousands of cats,

Millions and billions and trillions of cats.

Other favorites include the following.

Aardema, Verna. *Why Mosquitoes Buzz in People's Ears* with illus. by Leo and Diane Dillon (Dial, 1975).
    An African folktale rhythmically told and richly illustrated.

Bemelmans, Ludwig. *Madeline* with illus. by the author (Simon & Schuster, 1939).
    One of several stories about a high-spirited little French girl.

Caudill, Rebecca. *Did You Carry the Flag Today, Charlie?* with illus. by Nancy Grossman (Holt, 1966).
    A five-year-old has exciting experiences during a summer school session in the Appalachians.

Hoban, Russell. *Bedtime for Frances* with illus. by Lillian Hoban (Harper, 1960).
    Frances, the badger, like other little ones, hates to go to bed.

McGovern, Ann. *Too Much Noise* with illus. by Simms Taback (Houghton Mifflin, 1967).
    An old man troubled by too much noise in his house gets unusual advice from the village wise man.

Mosel, Arlene. *Tikki Tikki Tembo* with illus. by Blair Lent (Holt, 1968).
    A masterful retelling of an old Chinese tale.

Sawyer, Ruth. *Journey Cake, Ho!* with illus. by Robert McCloskey (Viking, 1953).
    An interesting twist to an old tale.

Sendak, Maurice. *Pierre* with illus. by the author (Harper, 1962).
    The story of a contrary little boy who learns to say, "I care!" One of four books of the Nutshell Library. The others are a book of months, an alphabet book in rhyme, and a counting book.

Slobodinka, Esphyr. *Caps for Sale* with illus. by the author (W. R. Scott, 1947).
    A timeless favorite that tells of a peddlar who lost his caps to mischievous monkeys.

Viorst, Judith. *Alexander and the Terrible, Horrible, No Good, Very Bad Day* with illus. by Raymond Cruz (Atheneum, 1972).
    Alexander learns that running away from bad days won't work.

Waber, Bernard. *Ira Sleeps Over* with illus. by the author (Houghton Mifflin, 1972).

A story of a first sleep-over told with sympathy in dialogue that echoes actual speech.

Stories for Older Children

Older children particularly enjoy well-drawn characters in humorous or perilous situations.

Atwater, Richard and Florence. *Mr. Popper's Penguins* with illus. by Robert Lawson (Little, Brown, 1938).

In a time-tested classic, Mr. Popper copes with penguins in a city home, with hilarious results.

Byars, Betsy. *The 18th. Emergency* with illus. by Robert Grossman (Viking, 1973).

Benjie angers the roughest boy in school and faces the consequences.

Cunningham, Julia. *Dorp Dead* with illus. by James Spanfeller (Pantheon, 1965).

Gilly encounters a modern monster in a thrilling tale of danger and escape.

Fleischman, Albert Sydney. *McBroom and the Beanstalk* with illus. by Walter Lorraine (Little, Brown, 1978).

McBroom's family suggests that he enter a contest for liars.

Lindgre, Astrid. *Pippi Longstocking,* trans. from the Swedish by Florence Lamborn, with illus. by Louis Glanzman (Viking, 1950).

Plucky Pippi never grows old and never loses her pep.

Myers, Walter. *The Dragon Takes a Wife* with illus. by Ann Grifalconi (Bobbs Merrill, 1972).

Harry the dragon seeks the help of an inept but lovely fairy in his fight against the knight.

Nostlinger, Christine. *Konrad,* trans. from the German by Anthea Bell, with illus. by Carol Nicklaus (Watts, 1977).

An original story about a boy made too perfect by his manufacturers.

O'Brien, Robert C. *Mrs. Frisby and the Rats of NIMH* with illus. by Zena Bernstein (Atheneum, 1971).

A group of literate rats set out to establish their own civilization.

Paterson, Katherine. *The Master Puppeteer* with illus. by Haru Wells (Crowell, 1976).

A story for mature listeners about a boy apprenticed to puppeteers.

ADDITIONAL SUGGESTIONS

Myths, folktales, and legends are excellent choices for reading aloud. A good source of these is an anthology of children's literature. The following anthologies, which feature fine retellings of old tales, are highly recommended:

Arbuthnot, May Hill, and Zena Sutherland. *The Arbuthnot Anthology,* 4th ed. (Scott, Foresman, 1976).
Johnson, Edna, and others. *Anthology of Children's Literature,* 5th ed. (Houghton Mifflin, 1977).

Tales by master storytellers such as Hans Christian Andersen and Rudyard Kipling may also be found in these anthologies or located from the sources listed in their extensive bibliographies, an outstanding feature of both the books listed above.

Although teachers on occasion may judiciously cut for various reasons bits from the texts they read aloud, abridged or simplified versions of works should be avoided. The style and language patterns of an author are an integral part of a story. When these patterns are altered, the integrity of the story is lost. Edited versions or insipid retellings, where language is simplified, are little more than summaries. The best translations, the finest versions of old tales, or the best contemporary retellings of them must be sought, and the original texts of writers like Kipling preserved intact.

Kipling's *Just-So Stories* are masterpieces of classic nonsense told in magnificent language that must be read or told "just so."

> . . . In the beginning of years, when the world was so new and all, and the Animals were just beginning to work for Man, there was a Camel, and he lived in the middle of a howling Desert because he did not want to work; and besides, he was a Howler himself. So he ate sticks and thorns and tamarisks and milkweed and prickles, most 'scruciating idle; and when anybody spoke to him he said "Humph!" Just "Humph!" and no more.*

*Rudyard Kipling, "How the Camel Got His Hump," *Just-So Stories,* illus. by J. M. Gleeson (Garden City, N.Y.: Doubleday, 1912), p. 15.

Independent Reading

Experiencing literature is the first step in becoming qualified to study it. Children can't talk about what they haven't experienced, nor can they connect works of literature with one another unless they are well read. Through television, comics, series books, and movies, most children are well educated in the sub-literary culture. What they are likely to lack, and therefore what the school must provide, is the experience of the best from among a wide variety of children's literature, old and new. Reading aloud provides some of this experience, but children need to develop the habit of reading for pleasure.

Many reading programs in elementary and middle school deal almost entirely with *how* to read. In these programs, centered often around reading machines, workbooks, and basal readers, little actual reading is accomplished. Yet, *what* children read and whether they read at all are concerns that educators must address. Skills, the *how* of reading, are useless unless they are applied. Children learn to read by reading and enjoying. Getting them to read is the challenging job of the adults in their lives. The success of a good reader is based as much on motivation as on skill.

Somehow, on a regular basis within the school schedule, time must be set aside for reading of real books and other natural reading material like periodicals. An independent reading program must parallel any program of instruction in basic skills. Indeed, some teachers believe that reading real books from the beginning is a better way to genuine literacy than engaging in the nonreading activities often associated with the kits, workbooks, and machines of reading laboratories.

At least half the time allotted for reading in school should be spent in individualized or independent reading, defined as reading for enjoyment or enlightenment books or periodicals the children choose for themselves.

An independent reading program begins with books and time in school to read them. Books may be borrowed for an extended period from the school or local library, purchased through children's book clubs (Scholastic Publishing Company operates an excellent one) or brought in from attics and basements. Once this classroom library is assembled, about three books to every child in the group, it needs a place of honor, even if it is only a milk-carton bookcase or display space on a table top. The library must include books that span a wide range of difficulty, from easy-to-reads to challenging novels for mature readers.

Books in the classroom library must be the best, those with literary merit as well as proven appeal. Librarians can supply information about what books are checked out most frequently by each age group (a list of selection aids is included later in this chapter). Discovering what is available in the field of children's literature is a research task that most teachers find pleasurable and personally rewarding.

Enthusiasm and genuine interest in the books are contagious. By giving book talks and reading aloud interesting excerpts from the books in the classroom library, teachers whet appetites for reading. By allowing time for brief responses to the question "Have you read a good book lately?" teachers let the children sell the books to each other.

In an independent reading program, the actual reading is what is important. The program need have no strings attached to it in the form of highly prescriptive lists of books to read or onerous reports to write. Record keeping on the children's part is of the simplest sort: titles and brief evaluative comments on index cards for others' reference.

Many teachers hold brief, individual conferences during independent reading sessions with those who have completed a book. These conferences are opportunities for students to share their experience of a book. Often they may wish to read aloud a preselected favorite portion of their book. This is not the time to relentlessly quiz children on what details of the book they recall, nor is there time in the conference to listen to drawn-out retellings of plot outlines.

It is often better to encourage objective comment on the book than to pry into a child's personal experience of it. Questions to prime response should direct the student's attention to the book itself and the literary elements of its construction. If, for instance, the teacher asks, "What is the book about?", the child's answer will probably be a comment on one or more of the elements of plot, character, setting, or theme. Other good general questions are: "Who tells this story?" "How does the story begin?" "How does it end?" "Was it the ending you expected?" (An extensive list of literary questions is found in Chapter 7.)

In launching a successful independent reading program, it is helpful to the students to give them a common experience through oral reading and subsequent guided discussion on the elements of stories in general. So prepared, independent readers proceed with greater confidence toward richer experiences with the books they read on their own. A short novel of high quality is useful for providing this experience in common. For third grade and up, the following short novels are excellent choices.

Cunningham, Julia. *Come to the Edge* (Pantheon, 1977).
   Embittered Gravel Winter learns to accept himself and others after he runs away from a home for foster children.

Estes, Eleanor. *The Hundred Dresses* (Harcourt, 1944).
   Classmates are belatedly sorry for their cruel treatment of a girl they find "different" from themselves.

Gardiner, John R. *Stone Fox* with illus. by Marcia Sewall (Crowell, 1980).
   Based on a Rocky Mountain legend, an action-filled story of courage and determination. Willie enters a bobsled race, hoping to win prize money to save his grandfather's farm.

Kennedy, Richard. *Inside My Feet: The Story of a Giant* with illus. by Ronald Himler (Harper, 1979).
   A thriller in which a child battles to save his parents when they are carried off by a giant's enchanted boots.

Pinkwater, Manus. *Wingman* with illus. by the author (Dodd, Mead, 1975).
   Donald Chen retreats from a school where he is the only Chinese and made to feel an outsider.

Richler, Mordecai. *Jacob Two-Two Meets the Hooded Fang* (Knopf, 1975).
   When he insults a grown-up, Jacob is sent to the Children's Prison where he encounters the Hooded Fang and other undesirables.

Steig, William. *The Real Thief* with illus. by the author (Farrar, 1973).
   The difficulty of admitting mistakes is gently handled in a story of guilt and friendship.

This book is primarily concerned with criticism that goes beyond response to individual works to examination of works in relation to each other. Before students are ready for a panoramic view of literature, however, they must experience and respond to large numbers of individual works.

Discussion as an Aid to Learning

Although the experience of each story is unique, stories have elements in common. To help students make the most of their independent reading, teachers can guide them through discussion of specific books. Guided study helps students to discover the common elements in stories and how these interrelate. As students learn how stories are constructed, their appreciation of them grows as well as their ability to create stories of their own.

Story Elements

The elements common to stories are *character, point of view, plot, setting, mood, language,* and *style.*

Discussion may focus on one or more of these elements at a time. These are among the understandings and abilities teachers want to help their students toward:

—An awareness of plot as a series of incidents or sequence of events through which the initial incident or story problem is resolved. In *Stone Fox,* the problem that sets the story going is the grandfather's illness and Willie's desire to have him well. Through the incidents of the plot, the problem is worked out.

—Skill in following story sequence and predicting possible outcomes. It is usually only after a story is experienced that readers can look back and note the clues or foreshadowings of the outcome supplied by the author. In the end, we are not surprised that Stone Fox has sympathy for a boy who wants to save his grandfather's farm from the tax collector; earlier in the book we learn that the Shoshone races to win money to buy back land for his tribe.

—Awareness of the tension between character and incident. Willie's characteristics of courage, determination, and industry, demonstrated *by* the incidents of the story, are in turn what make the *incidents* of *Stone Fox* possible and plausible.

—Ability to "read" character through appearance, relationship to the environment, actions, thoughts, speech, reactions *to* others, reactions *of* others. In building a three-dimensional study of a character, students should prove each descriptive statement about a character by direct reference to the text.

—Ability to note the mood or tone of a book. From the beginning, *Stone Fox* is optimistic, because Willie, its main character, expresses his optimism against all odds and his determination to change things for the better.

—Awareness of language as a means of establishing tone and mood. *Stone Fox* is a story of action told with a minimum of description and a considerable amount of dialogue. In *Come to the Edge* description of place and circumstance is relatively detailed so the reader shares in the effect these have on Gravel's feelings.

—Appreciation of humor, exaggeration, description, and figures of speech; the ability to form and react to the sensory images produced through language.

—Awareness of how setting, mood, and plot relate. The remote, desolate setting for *Inside My Feet* is necessary to sustain the mystery and strangeness of the plot.

An oral rather than a written response to the literature they read or listen to is more suitable for elementary and middle school students. At their stage of development, when extensive writing can be physically taxing, these young children are likely to regard written exercises such as character studies or plot summaries as punishment. To maintain interest in reading and to develop literary understandings, more is to be gained through guided group discussion.

In a planned discussion, children have the opportunity to express their ideas about literature, to test their notions against those of others, to become absorbed in study through active participation, to engage in both divergent and convergent thinking. The value of structured dialogue in the classroom cannot be overstressed. James Moffett describes adequate discussion as a *learned* process of

> amending, appending, diverging, converging, elaborating, summarizing, and many other things. Most of all, it is an external social process that each member gradually internalizes as a personal thought process: he begins to think in the ways his group talks. Not only does he take unto himself the vocabulary, usage, and syntax of others and synthesize new creations out of their various styles, points of view, and attitudes; he also structures his thinking into mental operations resembling the operations of the group interactions. If the group amends, challenges, elaborates, and qualifies together, each member begins to do so alone in his inner speech.*

Discussion that is structured and purposeful and at the same time free and relaxed facilitates the learning of specific literary

*James Moffett, *A Student-Centered Language Arts Curriculum, Grades K–6: A Handbook for Teachers* (Boston: Houghton Mifflin, 1968), p. 46: See also "Small-Group Discussion," in James Moffett and Betty Jane Wagner, *Student-Centered Language Arts and Reading, K–13: A Handbook for Teachers,* 3rd ed. (Boston: Houghton Mifflin, 1983), pp. 85–97.

concepts while it provides an opportunity for perfecting communication skills and being heard as an individual.

Guidelines for Successful Discussion

A distinction should be made between small- and large-group discussion. Whole-class discussion, unless it follows discussion by small groups, is unlikely to be more than an extemporaneous exchange among a few. Only a limited number of students in a class of average size can participate at once, comments are likely to be addressed to the teacher and not to other pupils, and unengaged minds are apt to wander. Children should be taught to discuss together in groups of no more than six or eight.

The process of discussion is something that must be *taught*; children cannot be expected to proceed with it profitably without specific guidance. Discussion has two major emphases: courtesy and participation. The child is introduced to the ritual exchange of give-and-take that genuine discussion requires. He learns to listen, to wait his turn, to assimilate and weigh what he has heard, and to build upon this when he speaks. The teacher works from the first encounter with a new class to establish a climate of mutual respect where ideas and opinions are courteously listened to, where one is helped toward understanding rather than criticized for the lack of it. The process is a developmental one with first experiences carefully planned for success.

With the teacher's guidance, the children themselves can evolve the ground rules that will govern their discussions. The first small-group activity for a class might well be a session in which groups work together to evolve these rules, pooling their ideas in a large-group sharing session at the end, and preparing a final list cooperatively for the guidance of all.

Discussion groups for literary criticism are likely to be best if they are heterogeneous and their composition frequently changed. Slow learners should have the opportunity to work with faster learners in an atmosphere of mutual help and support; the least articulate and the most verbally facile will mutually benefit from working together. Common interests, personal preferences, and individual needs will also determine the composition of groups. If there is a child as group leader, the role should be rotated.

At first the teacher may lead the discussion, working with a group while the rest of the class is engaged in other activities. Later he may circulate from group to group, working first with one and then another. As soon as possible he should abandon the role of leader and assume that of guide or resource person. Children should be encouraged to address their remarks to each other and not to the teacher when he joins their group.

As a guide and resource person the teacher has two functions: he helps to facilitate the group process itself and at the same time answers questions and supplies subject matter information the children may require. He should avoid offering quantities of unsolicited information, but he may, with judicious questioning, bring forth a request for information that he sees is needed. In facilitating the discussion process he gives the children needed experience in listening to hear each other out. Long-winded soliloquizers are good-naturedly curtailed; interruptions are discouraged with a tactful comment or hand gesture. As he visits each group, the teacher, with comments and questions: (a) encourages participation: "Mary, we haven't heard from you on this"; (b) handles the monopolizer with a tactful but firm comment such as "Wait a moment, John; Ruth hasn't finished yet"; (c) pacifies the one who has introduced an irrelevancy by suggesting that his idea should be noted for discussion at another time; (d) helps groups to draw conclusions and summarize their ideas; and (e) helps with definitional problems or more serious problems of personal relations. Throughout he provides a model for the students with his tact, courtesy, and genuine willingness to listen to another's ideas.

The more structured discussion may grow spontaneously from the comments and questions of the children. For example, after a fifth-grade class has heard a story, they might raise questions about the ending. A number feel strongly that "it couldn't have happened that way," that the author "fooled them," that "it doesn't make sense." The teacher might structure the ensuing discussion with: "Let's talk this problem over in smaller groups so everyone will get a chance to say what he thinks." (The teacher goes to the board.) "Now, what are some of the questions you have been asking? Let's jot down the main ones and you can try to answer them yourselves in your groups."

No discussion should be allowed to drag on interminably until the bored participants, talked out, turn to paper planes, spitballs, and harassment of others for solace. Three to five minutes will be sufficient for most questions, particularly in the beginning; but the experience, level of maturity, and interest of the class, as well as the purpose of the discussion, will be the teacher's guides in establishing time limits.

At the end of the small-group discussion, groups may be assembled together to pool ideas and *to evaluate their experience with the discussion process itself.* A leader or spokesman may report for the group; if groups have made use of recorders, the recorder might make the report, in more advanced classes making use of notes.

Each discussion should have a specific purpose to guide it or a specific problem to be discussed in the course of it. In structuring learning sequences in literary criticism by means of discussion, the teacher has the deductive scheme in mind to which the inductive presentation is related; the children reach an understanding of literary principles through a process of discovery that is facilitated by the interchange that the teacher guides and structures.

Principles into Procedure

In order to teach literature, the teacher must be a student of it. The understanding of the basic principles of literary theory is of little value without a broad knowledge of children's literature. To structure learning sequences the teacher needs to know what poems and stories will be best suited to each level. College courses in children's literature together with wide reading, ranging from picture books through novels written for early adolescents, will supply this knowledge. Reference books such as May Hill Arbuthnot's *Children and Books* are helpful but the information they supply is never a substitute for reading the literature itself. A collection of the calibre of *Anthology of Children's Literature* by Edna Johnson and others is useful in providing a perspective on the broad field of children's literature. Texts and anthologies like those mentioned provide comprehensive bibliographies of inestimable help to teachers in selecting their reading.

Other selection aids include *Adventuring with Books,* edited by Patricia Cianciola (Urbana, Ill.: National Council of Teachers of English, 1977), a resource that lists 2500 titles, chosen for literary quality, for preschool to eighth grade, and *The Bulletin of the Center for Children's Books* (Graduate Library School, University of Chicago, 5801 Ellis Avenue, Chicago, Ill. 60637), which reviews and rates children's books. For keeping abreast of new publications, *The Horn Book Magazine* (Park Square Building, 31 St. James Avenue, Boston, Mass. 02116), with its perceptive reviews, is invaluable.

To teach criticism it is not necessary to set up rigid courses of study to be "covered" in a given year. The literature used as examples in literary discussions and as the basis for creative response is all of the literature the children encounter, in school and out. It includes the books read independently by individuals and those shared through classroom reading. It includes the stories and poems selected by the teacher and shared with the whole group or smaller groups within it through reading aloud.

From the earliest age and through all the elementary grades children should be read to regularly, taking in literature by the ear as well as the eye. Children will never discover the wide and varied wonders to be found in literature by gazing at the spines of books in the library. They need the guidance of an interested, sympathetic adult who, by enthusiastically sharing all kinds of stories and poems, takes them well inside the vast world of literature. Left to themselves they are likely to explore only its outer boundaries or isolated areas here and there within it.

When literature is considered in terms of its structural principles, the approach to its study is broader and freer than study that centers in the content of individual works. It does not emphasize the close analysis of specific items in a prescribed text. It takes into account all of a student's reading and listening. The true business of criticism is not the pursuit of answers to a list of questions that test basic comprehension. Comprehension of literature occurs on many levels and some of it may not be translated into discursive language. Stories and poems must of course be understood in the sense of being intelligible. But it is unlikely that children will choose to read much that is incomprehensible to them. And it is unlikely that sensitive teachers will read to them for very long something that is above or beyond them. Criticism expands knowledge of literature in a natural way, giving the student the opportunity to think of literature in terms of all of his reading rather than merely in terms of items in a reader.

Criticism does not only involve the student's experience with literature. It means dealing with his total verbal experience as well. Much of this experience is sub-literary, found in television serials and advertisements, comics and magazines, films and pop songs. The points of contact between literary and sub-literary experiences need to be kept in mind, the whole considered in literary terms. Archetypal characters, images, and plots found in literature are found as well in sub-literary forms. Students who are helped to see these resemblances will be pleased to see that literature is not something that is associated only with classrooms. Furthermore, they will, by relating the two together, see how the mythology of television drama and advertisements copies that of literature. Through comparison they will gradually see how the one is a shoddy form, a rival mythology determined to capture their imaginations for its own purposes. Powers of discernment will not be developed all at once, but they will never be developed at all if children do not have an early awareness of how the mass media function to condition them.

Literary criticism, then, involves a consideration of all the literature a student encounters and all of his other verbal experience as well. In the next two chapters poetry and story are considered separately to facilitate the detailing of procedure in literary criticism. In actual practice they cannot be separated from each other, nor can they be separated from nonliterary experience. In genuine criticism the unity of literature is preserved and the scope of its influence made clear.

Chapter 6

The Study
of Poetry

Young children are natural poets. They *move* to language, skipping
or stomping or strutting to the rhythm of sounds. A six-year-old
hears a snatch of adult conversation and appropriates a word or
two, whirling his arms as he chants: "Involuted! Convoluted! Involuted! Convoluted!"

They savor words, tasting them, rolling them on their tongues
in the rhymes and jingles that are part of their games and communication with each other:

> Julius Caesar
> The Roman geezer,
> Squashed his wife with a
> lemon squeezer.*

To children rhyme is both funny and remarkable in itself. A
nine-year-old says of the following bit of nonsense, "I think what's
so clever about this is the way it all rhymes."

> Mrs. White had a fright
> In the middle of the night
> She saw a ghost eating toast
> Half-way up the lamp post.†

They are delighted by a word with two uses: "What runs but
never walks?" (*Answer:* A stream.) Puns of any kind please their
fancies, as do word plays and conundrums: "What is the difference
between a big black cloud and a lion with a toothache?" (*Answer:* One pours with rain and the other roars with pain.)

*Iona and Peter Opie, *The Lore and Language of School Children* (New York: Oxford
University Press, 1959), p. 20.
†*Ibid.*, p. 17.

79

Riddles are children's special delight. And riddles are like the metaphors of poetic thought: something is imaginatively described in terms of something else as the teeth and gums are in the following:

> Thirty white horses
> Upon a red hill
> Now they stamp,
> Now they chomp,
> Now they stand still.

In poetry language is tapped for rhythm, rhyme, double meanings, unusual juxtapositions of sound; it is used to create images. The best of poetry appeals directly to one or more of the senses. It is a concrete mode of expression as well as a remarkable and delightful one. Since their lore and daily language (chants, taunt-songs, word plays, and the like) show that children and poets have much in common, it is foolish—and dangerous—for teachers to deny children poetry. In school poetry is commonly regarded as a frill, an utter nonessential, and children are often deprived of it. This deprivation is evident in many children's dull, unrhythmic, graceless writing. The lilt, the surge and thunder of verse, the expert timing of the rise and fall of cadences, when they are absorbed over the course of time, do more to develop writing ability than books full of exercises.

In one experiment, children whose language classes for many weeks were devoted entirely to an *oral* reading of the *Iliad* in Richmond Lattimore's translation wrote "epic" poems of their own. One eleven-year-old, inspired by the historical novels of Rosemary Sutcliff that he had been reading, created an original plot centered around Marius, a young galley slave. An excerpt from his poem is proof that he had absorbed the rhythms and imagery of the *Iliad.*

> As he entered the hold, they sprang upon him,
> As lions spring upon the unwary buck,
> And they grappled with him and bound him.
> When morning dawned the boy awoke
> To feel sharp pain in his head
> Where they had struck him with a wooden club;
> Where bonds had been, there was now a shackle,
> And he was chained to a bench with others, unlucky,
> A slave in the galleys of
> King Solomon's Navy.

As the days became weeks,
And the weeks months,
He learned the ways of the rowers
From the man Jason, who was his friend.
So also he learned to eat the black bread;
And, as the jackals fight for the scraps
On the bony carcass that is left to them
By the lions, so he fought
For the scraps left to them by his master.
But, above all, he learned to hate.
    . . .

Laurence Woodruff

It may be difficult for those who are surrounded by masses of print that passes for prose to believe that any other mode of expression has validity. It will be even more difficult for them to believe that reading poetry is the best way to learn to write prose. Still, all teaching involves a certain measure of faith and there will be those willing to be persuaded.

They will be the ones who put poetry first, not last, in the language arts curriculum. In the interests of a balanced diet it will not be all the literary nourishment their students receive. But it will be served in large portions and never only as dessert.

Choosing Poetry for Children

There is one rule of thumb for the choice of poetry to be used with children: it should be the best available. It is essential that it be "poetic" in the sense of being imagistic and rhythmic. The work of chatty poets who write versified prose should be avoided as well as the nonpoetic verse that is written especially, and badly, for children in the form of sentimental ditties. Poems should employ metaphor and image effectively and delightfully; they should have strong sensory appeal; many should illustrate patterns of repetition and rhyme; all poems chosen for use with children should speak to the child at his level of understanding and experience, but they should also broaden experience and stretch the imagination with new concepts and fresh ways of looking at things.

Riddles are examples of pure imagery and they should have a central place at every grade level in the elementary school. In riddles and conundrums, rhymed or unrhymed, the poet's way of looking at the world is clearly evident; he uses analogy and association with telling effect. Early experience with epigrammatic sayings, concise and compact like the proverb, helps the child to understand the economy inherent in poetic expression. Many proverbs and epigrams are highly imagistic or metaphorical, illustrating at once two primary qualities of poetry.

Although it is the teacher's responsibility to bring the best of poetry to children, he should remember that he is choosing *for* children and, therefore, try to read and listen to poems as a child would read and listen. What delights a child may seem simplistic to the adult, but delight is an important ingredient in poetry programs for children. The wise teacher is one who learns from the pupils, encouraging them to share their own favorites whether they are from an anthology or from the oral lore of childhood: jingles, chants, game-songs, taunt-songs, word games, even the lively singing commercials learned from television and radio. Choosing poetry to use with children can never become an academic exercise.

Poems may be rhymed or unrhymed; they may be stories or lyrics; they may be old or new; they may be on any subject that might interest the children. Foolproof introductions to poetry are those that will lead the child to regard vigorous rhythm and metaphorical thought as a simple and direct form of utterance. Such introductions would include ballads; works suitable for children by such major poets as Emily Dickinson, William Blake, Christina Rossetti, and Gerard Manley Hopkins; and the work of modern writers of verse for children: Eleanor Farjeon, Walter de la Mare, David McCord, Harry Behn, Leland Jacobs, James Reeves, Dorothy Aldis, Laura E. Richards, and Eve Merriam, to name a few.

Poems may be classified in numerous ways. In anthologies they are grouped according to theme and content: nature poems, animal poems, poems about fairies, poems about love, poems about city life. When thinking in terms of archetypal criticism, however, the teacher will go beyond these arbitrary classifications to even broader ones. To foster the understanding of poems as part of the whole of literature, essentially the expression of man's search for identity between the objective and inner worlds of his experience, the teacher will consider poems as they fit into such classifications as these:

> —Poems that express wishes, dreams, and desires, usually of an existence or circumstance better than one presently being experienced.
> —Poems that deal with the life and death of humans, animals, birds, and nature.

—Poems that pinpoint a moment in time, a place, a wish, or desire.

—Poems that are simply expressions of feeling or emotion.

—Poems that are rhythmic and verbal representations of work or play.

Presenting Poetry to Children

Poetry as a Part of Daily Experience

When the little child is accepted as a rhythmic being, poetry will be seen and encouraged as a valid means of expression and not regarded as a mere frill or recreational activity for the time, free of the "real work" of the classroom. Poetry cannot be relegated to an occasional lesson in its appreciation. As Leland Jacobs, eminent educator and writer of children's verse, says, it must become an integral part of daily living, embedded in the ritual of the classroom. The effective teacher will have poems on the tip of his tongue for all occasions: if someone has new shoes, a new baby brother, or a case of the sniffles; if the first robin appears, or the first flake of snow, he will be ready at a moment's notice to bring forth an appropriate poem or know where to find one to read aloud.

The Importance of Oral Presentation

The infant who gets bounced on somebody's knee to the rhythm of "Ride a cock horse" does not need a footnote telling him that Banbury Cross is twenty miles northeast of Oxford. He does not need the information that "cross" and "horse" make (at least in the pronunciation he is most likely to hear) not a rhyme but an assonance. He does not need the value-judgment that the repetition of "horse" in the first two lines indicates a rather tin ear on the part of the composer. All he needs is to get bounced. If he is, he is beginning to develop a response to poetry in the place where it ought to start.*

In the elementary school years, and even before formal education begins, children should experience poetry orally. Children develop an antipathy toward poetry only after they become indepen-

*Northrop Frye, *The Well-Tempered Critic* (Bloomington: Indiana University Press, 1963), p. 25.

dent readers, when there is a greater possibility that poetry will become for them nothing more than static rows of print on a page, perhaps the subject of analysis and dissection, or something that they must memorize under pressure. The silent treatment of poetry can never result, at least for the young child, in an appreciation and enjoyment of poetry. Poetry should be read aloud, as effectively as possible, by the teacher, who in most cases will be the best oral interpreter the child will encounter. Recordings may be used for variety, but they are never a substitute for the live performance that involves direct sharing between a teacher and a class. Children should be encouraged but not coerced to read aloud to others, with preparation always preceding performance. All oral interpreters should prepare their presentations, selecting only those poems that they most enjoy, for these will be the best read.

As often as possible, the oral experience with poetry should be accompanied with a physical response. Children should repeat lines and verses that have natural appeal, perhaps joining in on the refrain as they listen to a verse such as:

> A farmer went trotting upon his grey mare,
>   Bumpety, bumpety, bump!
> With his daughter behind him so rosy and fair,
>   Lumpety, Lumpety, lump!
>
> A raven cried, Croak! and they all tumbled down,
>   Bumpety, bumpety, bump!
> The mare broke her knees and the farmer his crown,
>   Lumpety, lumpety, lump!
>
> The mischievous raven flew laughing away,
>   Bumpety, bumpety, bump!
> And vowed he would serve them the same the next day,
>   Lumpety, lumpety, lump!

Moving to the rhythms of the poem is to be encouraged. It is natural for little children to gallop to "Ride a cock horse," walk with "To market, to market," march smartly to "The Grand Old Duke of York," or hop in time with A. A. Milne's "Hoppity." For older children it is fun to act out the action words of a poem: "slink," "dance," "creep," "rush," and the like.

Poems may be acted out as well as moved to, their rhythmic qualities brought to life through physical response. The acting may be representational, with children taking turns miming each episode of, say, A. A. Milne's "The King's Breakfast," or it may be free movement, to a lyric such as Ella Young's "Rain."

> Dancing dancing down the street
> Comes the rain on silver feet:
> O hush, O hush,
> For the wind is fluting a song.
>
> Little flute of the wind,
> Little flute of the wind,
> Little flute of the wind
> Play on.
>
> Silver feet of the rain
> Come again, come again,
> Come with a fluting song.*

Avoiding Verse Vivisection

Poems should be respected and enjoyed for what they are—imaginative constructs that are not translatable into utilitarian prose. No effort should be made to extract what is often erroneously called a poem's "real" meaning.

The question, "What does it mean?" has no place in the study of poetry at any level, because it fails to make a necessary distinction between imaginative and discursive writing. What the poet meant to say is, literally, the poem itself; what he meant to say in any given passage is, in its literal meaning, part of the poem. It is a fruitless and wasteful procedure to translate or try to translate a poem into discursive commentary. Such teaching distorts the child's experience, giving him the confusing and erroneous belief that poetry exists only as a distortion of prose. Instead, the child should be helped to know, by means of the best examples and with enjoyment and experimentation, that poetry is a valid mode of thought. The poem is experienced as a whole, its "meaning" accepted as part of the whole.

Leland Jacobs, in his famous example of how a poem may be destroyed by treating it as discourse, quotes to classes of teachers "The Goblin" and mimics the absurdity of the misguided teacher who would ask his pupils such questions as "What does it mean?" "Where, children, does the goblin live?" "How many things does he do?" "Can you name each one in its proper order?"

---

*Ella Young, "Rain," in *Time for Poetry,* ed. May Hill Arbuthnot (Chicago: Scott, Foresman, 1952), p. 149.

THE GOBLIN

A goblin lives in *our* house, in *our* house, in *our* house,
A goblin lives in *our* house all the year round.
He bumps
And he jumps
And he thumps
And he stumps.
He knocks
And he rocks
And he rattles at the locks.
A goblin lives in *our* house, in *our* house, in *our* house,
A goblin lives in *our* house all the year round.

Rose Fyleman

If a poem requires considerable explication and commentary before, during, or after the reading of it, it is probably the wrong choice for a particular group. Poems should stand by themselves, requiring few if any props, at eye level with the child, representative or suggestive of something within his experience. Occasionally it may be necessary to clarify a concept or offer the meaning of a word before reading a poem to a class but, in general, even this practice should be avoided. A better plan is to encourage the children's own questions about points that may bewilder them.

The emphasis is upon delight rather than dissection. In Archibald MacLeish's words, "A poem should not mean but be." "It takes children a long time," say the Opies, "before they cease to be amazed that one word can have more than one meaning." Certainly a literary education worthy of the name should see to it that this amazement with the delightful things that words can do is fostered and made to last a lifetime. This can never be accomplished through unpalatable practices such as vivesection. Children's initial experiences with poetry must center in delight. Only if this is so are more analytical procedures possible and palatable as the child grows older. And even these must be planned to enhance and not destroy the essence of the poetic experience.

Archetypal Literary Criticism Applied to Poetry

Archetypes are the things which recur in literature and archetypal criticism . . . is an attempt to see what the literary context of a work of literature is . . . to see what

meaning can be thrown on the individual work from its
context in literature.*

A teacher of literature wants his pupils to experience poetry
with pleasure; he also wants their knowledge of literature to develop systematically. Although discursive explication and commentary about poems is to be avoided in the elementary school, this
does not mean that the young child's experiences with poetry cannot
be fitted meaningfully into a critical framework that will allow
his sense of literature as an order of words to grow and develop
with focus and direction. Through his *choice and arrangement* of
certain selections of poetry, the teacher can, through *guidance of
the children's questions and discussion,* help even the youngest child
to begin to see for himself how each poem is one of the larger family
of all literary works.

Significant learning takes place when the student goes beyond
a consideration of detail and specific content to become aware of
an overall pattern or structure to which he may relate discrete experiences. The student proceeds inductively, within a deductive
framework established by the teacher, to see relationships for himself. In the case of poetry, for instance, the teacher will help him
to see in what ways poetic expression is a unique mode of thought
with its own techniques and characteristics.

Discursive writing describes the world, but imaginative literature uses language in a way that connects our minds with the objective world in an effort to associate and identify the mind with what
goes on in the world beyond it. The simile and the metaphor are
the units of identification. They make of the objective world something that is essentially human in shape and try to recapture, in
words, man's original lost sense of identity with his surroundings.
The limit of the imagination is a totally human world where all
things are identical with man's mind or absorbed within it.

The logic of metaphor which insists that "this *is* that" is not
the logic of reason; it is, rather, an *imaginative* logic that illustrates
how the poet goes beyond nature to show a world absorbed and
possessed by the human mind. In poetry it is not only legitimate
but highly desirable to tell the "truth" by means of analogy and
association—truth that need not be defended or refuted in discursive terms because it cannot be. Poetry that makes use of associative language effectively with suggestive images that make their
own sense should be regarded by the child as a valid mode of expression. If he is able to grasp this basic understanding of poetry in

*Author's interview with Northrop Frye, August 27, 1970.

the elementary school, his problems of understanding or accepting the "difficult" images of the poets he will study in high school and beyond will be minimized.

Children should become aware of the logic of metaphorical language in literature, not by collecting similes and metaphors as if they were so many colorful pebbles, but by seeing for themselves, as they read and write, the worth and value of using concrete and sensory imagery to express ideas. Children employ metaphor in their natural expression and are skilled users of slang, which might be called the poetry of everyday speech. When their natural propensities are fostered and channeled and they are encouraged to make use of analogy and identity for precise expression, their own writing will benefit and they will take additional delight in the use of such expression by others.

A Learning Sequence for the Upper Elementary Grades

Aim of the sequence: In this example the teacher's principal aim is to lead the children to an understanding that certain patterns of imagery are associated with the expression of happy and sad feelings. The children have experienced a number of poems of their own and the teacher's choosing. Included in the teacher's selections might be poems like the following, representative of both moods and illustrative of the point he wants the children to grasp.

LAUGHING SONG

When the green woods laugh with the voice of joy,
And the dimpling stream runs laughing by;
When the air does laugh with our merry wit,
And the green hill laughs with the noise of it;

When the meadows laugh with lively green,
And the grasshopper laughs in the merry scene,
When Mary and Susan and Emily
With their sweet round mouths sing "Ha, Ha, He!"

When the painted birds laugh in the shade,
Where our table with cherries and nuts is spread,
Come live and be merry and join with me,
To sing the sweet chorus of "Ha, Ha, He!"

William Blake

HERE WE COME A-PIPING

Here we come a-piping,
In Springtime and in May;
Green fruit a-ripening,
And Winter fled away.
The Queen she sits upon the strand,
Fair as a lily, white as a wand;
Seven billows on the sea,
Horses riding fast and free,
And bells beyond the sand.

Traditional

CITY AUTUMN

The air breathes frost. A thin wind beats
Old dust and papers down gray streets
And blows brown leaves with curled-up edges
At frightened sparrows on window ledges.
A snow-flake falls like an errant feather:
A vagabond draws his cloak together,
And an old man totters past with a cane
Wondering if he'll see Spring again.

Joseph Moncure March

DARK GIRL

Easy on your drums,
Easy wind and rain,
And softer on your horns,
She will not dance again.

Come easy little leaves
Without a ghost of sound
From the China trees
To the fallow ground.

Easy, easy drums
And sweet leaves overhead,
Easy wind and rain;
Your dancing girl is dead.

Arna Bontemps

In Time of Silver Rain

In time of silver rain
The earth
Puts forth new life again,
Green grasses grow
And flowers lift their heads,
And over all the plain
The wonder spreads
    Of life,
    Of life,
    Of Life!

In time of silver rain
The butterflies
Lift silken wings
To catch a rainbow cry,
And trees put forth
New leaves to sing
In joy beneath the sky
As down the roadway
Passing boys and girls
Go singing, too,
In time of silver rain
    When spring
    And life
    Are new.

Langston Hughes

Discussion: The learning sequence proceeds as follows: the children have experienced a number of poems, and now, as preparation for writing their own, they are discussing them, the initial discussion involving the entire class. This is, of course, an "ideal" dialogue: these answers will not come so easily from most children. It shows the importance of the teacher's questions in eliciting responses.

Teacher: Think of the poems we have shared lately. What were some of the subjects they dealt with?
Pupils: —They talked about people.
       —And animals.
       —A lot of them were nature poems.
       —I think most of them expressed feelings.

—They all do! Every poem expresses some kind of feeling. That's what it's all about.

Teacher: What feelings do they express?

Pupils: —Sadness, sometimes, like in the poem "Dark Girl." It's gloomy, because, after all, she's dead.

—So is "City Autumn" sad. It makes you think of dreary days. There's not much hope in it.

—Most of the poems we heard were happy, though.

—Yeah. Like "Laughing Song" and that other one by Hughes, I think it was . . .

—I know. It's called "In Time of Silver Rain."

—Most of the poems we read by E. E. Cummings were happy, like the one that starts, "In just-spring."

—I guess you could say that most poems either make you feel sad or happy; some are stronger than others.

Teacher: Think of some of the happy poems you know. What season of the year are they usually describing?

Pupils: —Spring!

—Or summer!

—They're nearly always talking about the coming of spring or summer.

—The sadder poems are usually talking about fall, when the leaves are falling and things are dying. Like "City Autumn."

—Or it's winter and cold and everything is dead.

Teacher: Do you think you could arrange the poems you know according to the seasons?

Pupils: —All of them? Some of them don't mention a season.

—They may not mention one directly, but the idea is there.

—I think that's stretching it a little!

Teacher: Well, let's see if it is. *(The teacher sketches a circle on the board and divides it into four parts, labeling each respectively spring, summer, autumn, winter.*)* Why don't you get into groups of six: just pull your chairs

*This is illustrated in figure 3.1. It is important for students to realize that the purpose of this circle and the classifying of poems is *not simply to categorize them* but to reveal the images that *recur* throughout them all, differentiating them yet *uniting* them in one imaginative vision.

around in a circle with the people nearest you, and see whether you can classify the poems you know according to the four seasons, *whether they mention the seasons directly or not.* We'll pool your findings later.

Follow-up: The next learning sequence, evolving naturally out of this one, might be a consideration of the kinds of images from nature that are associated with happy poems and sad poems. Trees, gardens, fields, and flowers are associated with happy visions in most cases. Falling leaves, rocky landscapes, and harsh cold winds are usually associated with melancholy poems. The children might be asked what kind of images and what natural settings they would choose if they were going to write about death, say, or injustice, or pleasure and happy times.

A Learning Sequence for the Lower Elementary Grades

Aim of the sequence: Here the teacher leads young children toward an awareness that the literary imagination always seeks to suggest an identity between the human mind and the world outside it, and that it does so by means of metaphor, the language of identification: "This is that."

Discussion: Here again is an "ideal" dialogue with sample responses the teacher could try to elicit from students.

Teacher: Just before class I saw Peter galloping along the schoolyard.

Pupils: —I was a horse, a really fast race horse like the one I saw Saturday.
—It feels good to gallop.

Teacher: I'd like you all to act out for me what it's like to feel good. Let's push back the seats so we have room to move. Now, *show* me with your whole body what it's like to feel really good, really happy. *(Pupils proceed with movement mimes, some moving in place, others moving around the room.)* I saw lots of happy people just now. Mary, you seemed to be flying . . .

Pupils: —I was. I was a bird!

—I was a cloud!

—I was a rabbit and Tom was too; we were chasing each other.

—I was sunshine. Did you see me?

—I was a tree getting blown by the wind.

—I was flying a kite in the wind.

Teacher: Everybody acted out feeling happy by being something else. I wonder why?

Pupils: —That's just the way you do it.

—If I just stand here feeling happy, you couldn't really tell. I had to pretend I was a leaf flying around. That's what it feels like to be feeling good.

Teacher: Listen to this:

SWING SONG

Oh, I've discovered
A happy thing!
For every game
There's a song to sing,
Sometimes with words
Sometimes without,
It's easy to tell
What a song's about
From only a humming
Like wind at noon,
It needn't be even
Half a tune
If only it goes
With what you do,
If what you do
Is exactly true,
Or anyway if
It seems to you.
The time I discovered
This wonderful thing
I really was swinging
In a swing.
And the song I was singing
Was just as true

For all the flying
Sky-things too,
For seagulls and eagulls
And bees and bugs
And arrows and sparrows,
Enchanted rugs,
Clouds and balloons,
Balloons and bees—
A backward humming
A forward breeze,
Swinging without
Any tune you please.

Harry Behn

Pupils: —Feeling happy is like swinging on a swing.
—It's like a song going on inside you.
—Like the poem we know about the kite.

Teacher: Will you all say that one for me? I'll start and you join
in. *(They say together the following little poem that they
have learned.)*

A KITE

I often sit and wish that I
Could be a kite up in the sky,
And ride upon the breeze and go
Whichever way I chanced to blow.*

Teacher: In order to show what it's like to feel happy, you have
to use a comparison. Feeling happy is like other things.
Is that what you're telling me? *(Teacher records re-
sponses on the board, on a chart, or on tape.)*
Pupils: —Yes! Feeling happy is humming a song.
—Feeling happy is a bird.
—Happy is sunshine.
—Happy is wind.
—Happy is butterflies in your stomach.
—Happy is like a big red balloon.

Teacher: Do you know what? You've made a poem just by saying
what happy is like. You did just what the poets do. Do
you know what I mean by that?

*Author unknown. Arbuthnot, ed., *Time for Poetry,* p. 143.

Pupils: —We said that things were like other things.
　　　　　—We said things *were* other things.
　　　　　—We said a feeling like happy was like something you
　　　　　　can smell.
　　　　　—Or hear.
　　　　　—Or even taste.
Teacher: Let's read our poem.

Follow-up: Subsequent learning sequences would further develop the idea of metaphor to identify things other than emotions. The book *Hailstones and Halibut Bones* and the film made from the book would be suitable literary material for this purpose, used to teach the concept of metaphor and to stimulate similar compositions by the children.* The following is an excerpt from *Hailstones and Halibut Bones:*

WHAT IS WHITE?

White is a dove
And lily of the valley
And a puddle of milk
Spilled in an alley—
A ship's sail
A kite's tail
A wedding veil
Hailstones and
Halibut bones
And some people's telephones.

Mary LeDuc O'Neill

Structuring Additional
Learning Sequences with Poetry

Imagery I: Selected poems will help the children to see that many poems are involved with wishes, dreams, and desires. The teacher's stimulus for such a sequence would include questions such as the following: *What kinds of things do people wish for? When we think of things becoming better than they are, what direction do we associate with "getting better," down or up? What seasons of the year or times of day are usually associated with getting one's*

*The film is available, for purchase only, from Sterling Educational Films, 241 E. 34th St., New York, N.Y. 10016.

wish or realizing a dream? Poems such as the following might be included in the learning sequence:

HAIKU

When my canary
flew away, that was the end
of spring in my house.

WILD GEESE

I heard the wild geese flying
   In the dead of night,
With beat of wings and crying
   I heard the wild geese flying,
And dreams in my heart sighing
   Followed their northward flight.
I hear the wild geese flying
   In the dead of night.

Elinor Chipp

UP IN THE AIR

Zooming across the sky
Like a great bird you fly,
      Airplane,
      Silvery white
      In the light

Turning and twisting in air,
When shall I ever be there,
      Airplane,
      Piloting you
      Far in the blue?

James E. Tippett

FIREFLY

A little light is going by,
Is going up to see the sky,
A little light with wings.

I never could have thought of it.
To have a little bug all lit
And made to go on wings.

Elizabeth Madox Roberts

STARS

O, sweep of stars over Harlem Streets
O, little breath of oblivion that is night.
          A city building
          To a mother's song.
          A city dreaming
          To a lullaby.
Reach up your hand, dark boy, and take a star.
Out of the little breath of oblivion
          That is night
          Take just
          One star.

Langston Hughes

ROADS GO EVER EVER ON

Roads go ever ever on,
Over rock and under tree,
By caves where never sun has shone,
By streams that never find the sea;
Over snow by winter sown,
And through the merry flowers of June,
Over grass and over stone,
And under mountains in the moon.

J. R. R. Tolkien

DECEMBER

A little boy stood on the corner
And shoveled bits of dirty, soggy snow
Into the sewer—
With a jagged piece of tin.
He was helping spring come.

Sanderson Vanderbilt

Imagery II: Man's "dreams" and "nightmares" may be examined through his poetry. The teacher's questions to stimulate this learning sequence might include: *What images of nature are associated with happy dreams? with nightmares? What seasons and times of day are associated with dreams? with nightmares? Of the city and the country, which place is likely to be associated with dreams? with nightmares?* Poems such as the following would be included in the learning sequence:

A CITY PARK

Timidly
Against a background of brick tenements
Some trees spread their branches skyward.
They are thin and sapless,
They are bent and weary—
Tamed with captivity;
And they huddle behind the fence
Swaying helplessly before the wind,
Forward and backward
Like a group of panicky deer
Caught in a cage.

Alter Brody

TRANSCONTINENT

Where the cities end, the
dumps grow the oil-can shacks
from Portland, Maine,

to Seattle. Broken
cars rust in Troy, New York,
and Cleveland Heights.

On the train, the people
eat candy bars, and watch,
or fall asleep.

When they look outside and
see the cars and shacks, they know
they're nearly there.

Donald Hall

HEAVEN–HAVEN

I have desired to go
     Where springs not fail,
To fields where flies no sharp and sided hail
     And a few lilies blow.

And I have asked to be
     Where no storms come,
Where the green swell is in the havens dumb,
     And out of the swing of the sea.

Gerard Manley Hopkins

HEAVEN

Heaven is
The place where
Happiness is
Everywhere.

Animals
And birds sing—
As does
Everything.

To each stone,
"How-do-you-do?"
Stone answers back,
"Well! And you?"

Langston Hughes

THINGS TO REMEMBER

The buttercups in May
The wild rose on the spray
The poppy in the hay

The primrose in the dell
The freckled foxglove bell,
The honeysuckle's smell

Are things I would remember
When cheerless, raw November
Makes room for dark December.

James Reeves

Rhythm: The teacher may feel that a number of children's poems do not fit into the cyclical or dialectical image patterns. These are the rhythmic poems and chants that are analogous to the work songs and lullabies of adult poetry. Two examples follow:

Hush, little baby, don't say a word,
Papa's going to buy you a mocking bird.

If the mocking bird won't sing,
Papa's going to buy you a diamond ring.

If the diamond ring turns to brass,
Papa's going to buy you a looking-glass.

If the looking-glass gets broke,
Papa's going to buy you a billy-goat.

If that billy-goat runs away,
Papa's going to buy you another today.*

Traditional

THE PICKETY FENCE

The pickety fence
The pickety fence
Give it a lick it's
The pickety fence
Give it a lick it's
A clickety fence
Give it a lick it's
A lickety fence
Give it a lick
Give it a lick
Give it a lick
With a rickety stick
Pickety
Pickety
Pickety
Pick.

David McCord

Poems such as these are best experienced in situations that provide opportunity for physical response: movement to the rhythms, miming the action and the rhythm, speaking the words chorally, setting them to music for singing, and the like. With such poems an active participation in their rhythms and a delight in repetitions, rhymes, and word plays for their own sake are what constitute criticism for the young child.

*Iona and Peter Opie, *The Oxford Nursery Rhyme Book* (New York: Oxford University Press, 1955), p. 18.

Chapter 7

The Study of Story

> One essential aspect of literary training, and one that
> it is possible to acquire, or begin acquiring, in childhood,
> is the art of listening to stories. This sounds like a passive
> ability, but it is not passive at all: it is what the army
> would call a basic training for the imagination.
>
> NORTHROP FRYE*

Discourse and Non-Discourse

In addition to experience with poetry, the young child's literary
education includes prose, particularly the prose of story rather than
of discourse. A clear line should be drawn between discursive and
non-discursive writing in the literary experience of the child. Imaginative structures should be experienced first as they are, with no
attempt to "translate" them into discursive language. In Northrop
Frye's words:

> I keep insisting on capitalizing on and exploiting a small child's
> attention when you're telling him a story, because to hold that
> attention until the story is told is a very rare mental achievement
> for an adult. Children can do it, and if you can persuade a child
> to keep on doing it, he won't have any trouble with literature.
> But, instead, children get switched over to the values of the prose
> civilization and the conception of content so that they are trained
> to look at every work of literature, or at paintings, for that matter,
> or even music, and to say: "What's in it for me?" "What can I

*"The Developing Imagination," *Learning in Language and Literature*, A. R. Mac-
Kinnon and Northrop Frye (Cambridge: Harvard University Press, 1963), p. 43.

101

grab and carry off?" They look at a poem or painting and say: "What does it mean?" "Explain it to me so I can get something out of it." But the very simple childish response of staring at a picture or being absorbed in a poem as a whole is exactly what the painter or poet wants you to do.*

Stories requiring little or no explication or commentary should be chosen and presented as entities. In listening to or reading a story as an entity the child's mind is directed toward total structure rather than snippets of content. The whole design of a literary work is comprehended only when it is experienced as a whole. Furthermore, children should be encouraged to hear a story out before questioning it. Those who may make objections to talking pigs and airborne carpets are confusing discursive and imaginative writing. Stories are to be accepted as stories. Children should be invited to hear them through, making no attempt to judge them in terms of external standards of "truth" as though they were factual or informational writing. As Coleridge suggested, we need to acquire "a willing suspension of disbelief."

A work of literature is a body of hypothetical thought and action, expressing not what happened but what *happens,* in Aristotle's sense of the typical, recurrent, universal event. Questions about literature should turn in on the literature itself, with no attempt to test its "truth" against external correspondences. We do not ask: Is it true that there is a Yellow Brick Road? but: Is it imaginatively conceivable that there could be?

Asking Literary Questions

Thus, the first act of literary criticism is a simple one. Stories are read or listened to as stories. If there are questions, they should come from the children. Even these should be guided so that children come to think of content in terms of structure and form rather than in relationship to something extraneous to the story. If the child inquires, for example, why the story ended as it did or why a character behaved in a certain way, the teacher will *take him back into the story itself to find the answer.* Irrelevant questions are those that ask, "Did the boy behave as you would?" "What would you have done had you been in his place?" and the like because their answers lead the child outside of the story and align its "meaning" with external meanings.

*Author's interview with Northrop Frye, January 12, 1970.

Content, in the discussion of literature, cannot, of course, be ignored. However, we should try to talk about content as far as possible in terms of form and structure. If, as an example, the child says: "I don't like the way the writer makes the boy behave," it might be profitable to say, "Well, write a story of your own or rewrite this one and work out his behavior to suit yourself." Such an exercise, when practical, would help the child to see that a character's behavior need not always be considered in terms of its moral implications. A character often behaves the way he does in order for the story to develop along certain lines; characters may, in fact, be examined *structurally.* To use an example from children's literature: Templeton the rat, in E. B. White's *Charlotte's Web,* may not be a thoroughly desirable character, but he serves the purpose of the plot precisely because he *is* undesirable.

Questions that begin with "Why?" are to be encouraged, because they direct the child to a consideration of the reasons the author used a particular technique. What is bad pedagogically is to make the child remember what is said in a passage. What is right pedagogically is the asking of questions like "Why did he say it in this way?" The children as critics should not be bogged down with the memorization of factual detail related to stories they read and hear. The aim is to guide them to see relationships, patterns, and analogies among many stories and literary experiences, not to transfix them in the detailed examination of a single story, even though that story is first considered as an entity.

Content is an aspect of story that cannot, of course, be divorced from form and structure, but neither should form and structure be sacrificed wholly to content. A story first and always provides pleasure or involvement for a reader-listener. It should not be used for any other purpose. Stories, good and bad, will incidentally present values and offer vicarious and perhaps broadening experience. They are, however, *story* first and foremost. Children should be discouraged from reading stories for messages and morals or miscellaneous general knowledge, however valuable all of these may be. *The Tale of Peter Rabbit,* for example, may be seen as having a very definite moral. Read one way it teaches that if you disobey your mother you may be endangered, lose your clothes, feel ill, and be sent to bed with medication. Another valid interpretation might be that disobedience means an active and exciting life. In either case, the literary point of the story is missed; for the tale of Peter is the classic adventure story of romance, with Peter, the typical hero, home triumphant—albeit a little sick to his stomach—after successfully completing a quest.

Content, then, should be discussed as far as possible in terms of form and structure. This approach facilitates many of the understandings we want to develop in beginning literary critics. If the child examines form and structure, he will become aware that stories come in a certain limited number of conventional shapes and that certain patterns of imagery are common to different types of story. He will begin to see the patterns in story: how major and minor characters relate and reveal themselves through the design of situation and incident. Here are some examples of questions that deal with story content in terms of form and structure.

Type of Story

—Every storyteller constructs a make-believe world that may be very like our own or entirely different from it. What signs and signals indicate whether a story will be more fanciful than realistic? (Talking animals; exaggeration; strange, improbable situations, characters, or settings; stories that begin: "Once upon a time . . .")
—If the word created by the author is far different from the world we know, how does the author make the story seem possible and believable? (The author creates the world down to its last detail. For example, C. S. Lewis gives his magical Land of Narnia a complete geography, with land forms, plants, and weather.)

Setting and Plot

—Where and when does the story take place? How do you know? If the story took place somewhere else or in a different time, how would it be changed? (Readers will recognize that specific time and place are less important to some stories than others.)
—What incident, problem, conflict, or situation does the author use to get the story started? (Here readers and listeners focus on form, recognizing that a story begins at a particular point, usually with conflict, and moves to a middle and an end.)
—What does the author do to create suspense, to make you want to read on to find out what happens? (Sets up a situation that must be resolved; holds back the resolution through providing dramatic scenes that delay the resolution but lead inevitably toward it; keeps you guessing as to the nature of the resolution.)
—How is the story arranged? (Chronological order; individual incidents; flashbacks; told through letters or diary entries.)

—Trace the main events of the story. Is it possible to change their order? Leave any of them out? Why or why not? (A well-constructed story develops organically, action developing out of previous action.)

—Suppose you thought of a different ending for the story. How would the rest of the story have to be changed to fit the new ending? (Consideration of this question helps readers to recognize unity in structure; a story is an organic whole, the ending inevitable, given its beginning and middle.)

—Did the story end as you expected it to? What clues did the author offer to prepare you to expect this ending? Did you recognize these clues as important to the story as you were first reading or listening to it? (Clues, *foreshadowings* of what is to come, are often not apparent to inexperienced readers until the reading is complete. How subtly they are used is a mark of the author's skill and a structural aspect of story interesting to study.)

Characters

—Who is the main character in the story? What kind of person is this character? How do you know? (Through description, through the character's behavior, through what the character says and what others say about the character. Good writers reveal characters by *showing* what they are like rather than telling about them.)

—Are any characters changed in the course of the story? If so, how are they different? What changed them? Does the change seem believable? (Readers see how, through incident and experience, characters change and develop; good storytellers make the change believable and inevitable. Some signs of a possible change are in the character from the beginning.)

—Some characters play small but important roles in a story. Pick out a bit player from the story. Why is this character necessary to the story? (Minor characters act as foils, helping the reader to see a main character clearly through contrast, for instance. Often minor characters are used to move a plot forward.)

Point of View

—Who is the teller of the story? If the teller is a character in the story, how is the story different from one told by an outside narrator? (Readers can begin to consider "point of view," discussing the relative advantages and disadvantages of telling a story in first or third person.)

Mood and Theme

—Does the story as a whole create a definite mood or feeling? What is the mood? How is it created? (Descriptions, particularly of settings, create mood; a lighthearted tone may be established through dialogue or when a character embarks on a trivial quest; a serious tone is set when a quest involves life and death.)
—Did you have strong feelings as you read the story? (Anger, delight, joy, fear, sorrow, sympathy.) What did the author do to make you feel strongly? (Created sympathetic characters believably and placed them in dramatic situations, making readers experience along with them and therefore care about what happens to them.)
—What are the main ideas *behind* the story? (Survival, injustice, search for identity, brotherly love, courage, loyalty, love conquers all.) How does the author get you to think of them? (In a good story, thematic lessons are presented indirectly, through dramatic action of interesting characters.)

General Questions

—Is this story, though different in content, like any other story you have read or watched? Does it follow a pattern? If so, what is it? (A journey or quest, a struggle or predicament that is resolved by magical intervention, a series of episodes of equal importance, etc.)
—Think about the characters in the story. Are any of them the same character types you have met in other stories? (Brave, successful hero or heroine, wise adviser, villain, etc.)

Comprehension and Response

Checking Comprehension

Many teachers seem to feel that theirs are the only valid questions to be asked in the classroom. In a nervous effort to check basic comprehension of a story, or to have the children see it from *their point of view,* teachers are likely to isolate such parts of the whole as sequence of events or descriptive detail and make this the subject of questioning. Or they assign the kiss of death: the book report. Since story is quite unlike discursive writing from which specific information and facts may be extracted, it is inappropriate to test whether the child has understood a story by a series of questions that treat the story as informational writing. There are many ways to understand a story and they are *not all translatable* into descriptive prose. A more appropriate test of the child's comprehension of the stories he reads and hears is an artistic or creative response.

After a story is read, children, individually or in groups, have at their disposal a variety of creative responses. Through their dramatizations they will demonstrate whether they have grasped characterization, sequence of events, mood, and the like. Through art work related to the story, they will indicate their grasp of the same elements in addition to details about setting and the depth of their imaginative grasp of the story.

Dramatizations: Pantomime is an effective means of acting out a story. Creating *tableaux* (still, mimed pictures) to tell a story works well with small groups within a class. To prepare a series of tableaux, children who have read or heard the same story decide which key incidents need to be mimed and in what order. To select the key events and place them in their correct sequence requires full comprehension of a story and judgment about the relative importance of story incidents.

(Some teachers save space in their classrooms for dress-up materials to use in dramatizations: old wigs, a cape, a wooden sword or two, a selection of hats, a shawl, and perhaps a pair of high boots.)

Puppets delight children and provide an alternative means of acting out stories. Puppets are best when they can be simply and quickly made for instant use. A paper circle, painted or decorated with colored paper to resemble a character's face and fastened to a ruler, is an effective puppet. In preparing a story or scene for a puppet presentation, children are required to tell the story through dialogue alone. In doing so, they learn about the function of both narration and dialogue.

Art Work: Responses to literature through drawing, painting, and sculpting in clay are pleasurable tasks that help children recreate their literary experience with clarity and specificity.

Making original book jackets with illustrations and flap material or creating posters to advertise a book are activities enjoyed by most children. Montages and collages are excellent group activities. Children add scenes from the books they have read to make their collective effort an attractive record of what they all have read. Cutouts of book characters, drawn by the children, may be used together with memorable quotations from stories to build up a montage.

Cardboard mobiles may be used to illustrate books. On the various sections (oblongs, squares, triangles, circles, or free forms) of the mobile, suspended from a central piece and from each other with thread, artists draw key scenes from their books.

A series of drawings or transparencies for the overhead projector may be used to recreate the main incidents of a story or provide background for a dramatization.

The Critical Response

The creative response to literature is, of course, more than a test of comprehension. It constitutes a major aspect of the entire critical process. If the child is able to act out the key scenes of a story he has heard, he is aware of the structure of that story; if he is able to make a picture of a character or scene from a book, he has been able to visualize what he has read or heard; if he is able to write an episode making use of a character in a story, he has been able to grasp the details that make up that character.

In the young child a valid critical response may be more basic than creative. He may wriggle with delight or wiggle in boredom. He may sigh or gasp or join in on a refrain. He may ask to hear the story "one more time" or go off, starry-eyed, clutching the book it was read from.

Presenting Stories to Children

The actual study of literature has traditionally been reserved for older students or elementary students who are considered to be superior readers and reasoners. If a child is a slow learner, it is commonly believed that he has only time for learning the basic communication skills and little time for anything that is not strictly utilitarian. This elitist approach to literary studies is nonsense, not to mention its being anti-humanistic. The less intellectually gifted child should not be deprived of literature while he receives extra instruction in the practical and utilitarian uses of language. Even the dullest child will profit from imaginative "basic training": he can listen to stories and poems, even though he may not be able to read them independently.

The child understands with ear and heart what may be beyond the reach of his eye as a reader. Story "reading" competency may, therefore, be developed with the youngest children and with those who are not independent readers, for stories may always be presented orally by someone who does read independently. They may also be presented through pictures such as film strips, or through films. Dramatization is yet another form of presentation for story, valued for its own sake, and because it may be used when decoding skills are absent or minimal. An oral or visual presentation, or a combination of the two, allows all pupils, whether they read independently or not, to become absorbed effortlessly in a story as a whole and so be able to grasp its total structure. An oral presentation has another factor to recommend it—it allows the children to hear the storyteller's "voice." The printed form of a story is merely an echo of that voice and must be interpreted as effectively and vividly as possible if it is to be brought fully to life. Fine stories, like poetry, are meant to be heard; their rhythms provide memorable linguistic patterns to be absorbed by the children.

Children should experience the widest possible variety of stories: myths, Bible tales told as stories, legends, tales of the heroes of epic and romance, folk and fairy tales, fables, realistic stories, fantasy, and all the rest. Story means novels, short stories, and tales; or excerpts from book-length stories or novels, if they are selected for the quality of their story within a story.

Most stories for children, until the last few years, have been comic or romantic in shape. Recently, however, realistic stories in the ironic mode dominating the adult literary scene have had an influence on children's literature. Although it is true that young children seem to respond well to the comic and romantic structures, older children of today respond equally well to ironic and, to a lesser extent, satiric parodies of these structures. There are, at any rate, elements of both tragedy and irony in children's stories beginning with Humpty Dumpty's disastrous end and the ironic comeuppances experienced by the indomitable Punch of Punch and Judy, who invariably, after triumphantly besting everyone in sight, is himself annihilated by the one enemy he failed to foil. Stories in all four of the modes, or stories that contain elements of all four modes, should be included in a well-balanced curriculum for today's children, if their elementary experience is to prepare them adequately for literary encounters at more sophisticated levels by making them as insightful as they can be *right now.*

All through the elementary school a student should become gradually aware that stories come in certain conventional shapes. As he becomes familiar with a variety of stories, even the youngest child notes formal similarities among them. He anticipates events: "The 'good guy' will catch the 'bad guy' 'cause 'good guys' always win." He learns to predict outcomes by sizing up beginnings: "It starts 'Once upon a time' so it's a 'lived-happily-ever-after' story." "It starts with trouble but it looks like the hero can solve the problem so it will end happy." With experience of stories he learns to distinguish "Believe" from "Make-Believe" by their very different qualities.

The fundamental literary patterns and conventions derived from myth and ritual are best seen in literature like the epic, the saga, and the fairy tale. In the traditional narrative a king or hero goes forth to engage in a contest or combat, his story clearly illustrating a pattern basic to literature, the quest. Vestiges of the ancient myths and rituals persist in traditional stories. Legends, epics, fairy tales, and the like are concerned primarily with supernatural beings, kings, and heroes, as were the rituals that gave birth to them. In ritual drama it was common for a man, disguised as an animal, to speak or to suddenly remove his animal disguise and appear as himself. Storytellers are steeped in story, their stories growing out of other stories consciously and unconsciously. The quest as a plot design, characters like kings and heroes, conventions like transformations and talking animals recur in tales that provide readers and hearers with a sense of the venerability of story structure and convention. Traditional literature is to literature what still life is to painting: studies in basic form. The old tales form a basis for evaluating the structure of all subsequent stories.

The traditional stories of a culture also put the child in contact with many of the "social myths" that have figured in the development of his society. Every society has a central group of stories that inform not only its literature but other aspects of its social life as well. The major myths explain the origin of social classes; they account for rituals and the like. A knowledge of them through literature can make social life more intelligible. Literary works that express these informing social myths most clearly are works that should receive the educator's attention, whenever it is possible to use them. They are not invariably the books of greatest literary value. Included among them are stories of the Horatio Alger type, celebrating virtuous behavior and enterprise as means to financial and social success, and stories that contain more modern "myths" as they show the tuned-out or turned-off youth seeking value within himself as he rejects the value systems of his parents.

The child's literary experience includes the old and new, the "bad" and "good," the stories encountered in school and those encountered out of it. A "good" story is a well-constructed story, since the problems the artist has in beginning, developing, and concluding his story are problems that will exist as long as stories are told.

The question of what is morally suitable or unsuitable for children's consumption is inappropriate for consideration here, except to say that it is virtually impossible to protect children entirely from stories whose content, from an adult viewpoint, is undesirable for them. Questions of desirability usually turn on matters of content rather than structure. If children were to consider story *first as story* in school and direct their attention to structure and form *before* content, they might well be developing an immunity to the effects of unwholesomeness in stories. Certainly, if their critical endeavors are centered in a consideration of form and structure, they will be able to evaluate all of the stories they encounter. They will learn for themselves how certain movies, television dramas, and children's serials in book form are weak structurally— predictable, lacking in character motivation, making use of heavy manipulation of incident for effect. Both the mediocre and excellent are part of the child's literary experience, for almost all children watch television, read comics, and delight in series books at one time or another, and it is to be hoped that their school experience would provide them with some of the best possible literary encounters. It is only through wide exposure to the best, the mediocre, and the worst that the child will eventually develop taste and judgment as well as critical astuteness.

It is important that the child have as mixed a bag as possible, folk tales and the like, modern realistic stories, and fantasy. Modern stories are essentially "displacements" of the basic story patterns. The Cinderella story, for example, is in the comic mode: the archetypal pattern for the very latest "success story" with its sudden reversal of fortune that culminates, often miraculously, in a happy ending. Because they employ the pattern of the successful quest of the hero, the Old Testament story of David's triumph over Goliath and the modern picture book that shows a little boy coping with the modern "giants" of his experience are in the same romantic mode.

The young literary critic reads and hears a wide variety of stories as stories. This is the first step along the critical path. Avoiding personal value judgments and abstract analysis, criticism for children is centered in imaginative response; within a deductive framework supplied by the teacher, the child works inductively to make analogies, note resemblances, and relate all aspects of his literary experience from folk tales to modern novels.

Since the best of literature is not written with a controlled vocabulary or with particular attention to length or structure of sentences, the age-grade label attached to many stories may safely be removed. Where children cannot read the stories for themselves, the teacher can read aloud to them. As a professional aware of the needs and the level of ability of a particular class, the teacher will make choices in accordance with his pupils' best interests, always bearing in mind that it is his responsibility to foster new interests and broaden literary experience.

Obviously some stories, because of their content, length, and structure, are eminently more suited for use with kindergarten to third grade than others: nursery tales like "The Three Bears," "The Three Pigs," "Henny Penny," and "The Gingerbread Boy"; and picture story books with their simple vocabularly and repetitive patterns, such as Wanda Gág's *Millions of Cats,* Barbara Emberley's *Drummer Hoff,* and Harve Zemach's *The Judge.* Folk and fairy tales, tales of the heroes of epic and romance, and book-length stories are for grades four to six. But the designation of grade level in the case of literature can never be rigidly adhered to. Little children, for instance, will readily grasp a telling or reading of a simple version of the Moses story, while a more complex version of the tale, with the text taken from the Bible, would be reserved for older children.

Archetypal criticism, with its look at the broad patterns in literature, does not limit the teacher to a list of stories by grade, a classification that is always arbitrary and restricting. A good story bears a second or even third retelling, as all teachers, librarians, and parents well know. Stories children have read or encountered in some form in other years will form part of their critical discussions. The cry of "We've had this before" is to be welcomed rather than feared and avoided, for former exposure can be turned to good use when children are considering stories not merely as separate entities, but as parts of the whole universe of story and poetry. They will be encouraged to review or remember stories encountered earlier for the sake of comparison: to note similarities of structural patterns, to see how the same type of character turns up again and again, to note recurrent patterns of imagery and symbolism.

Archetypal Literary Criticism
Applied to Story

The practice of archetypal criticism involves a stepping back from the individual poem or story to see it in the context of literature as a whole, as one of a family of stories and poems: a literary universe. It is taken for granted that the archetypal critic has mastered the story-reading abilities appropriate to his level of maturity. He can listen to a story all the way through, holding in his mind sequence of events, relationships among characters, and significant detail; he is able to make inferences and predict outcomes; he is alert to nuances in tone and mood. These and other basic abilities in story reading are developed progressively as each new story is encountered in the classroom. In addition, the teacher structures learning sequences that allow the children to consider individual stories in relationship to others and as part of the whole universe of literature. Simulations of the discussion portions of a number of learning sequences are presented on the following pages as examples. They show how basic critical understandings may be fostered by a process of inductive reasoning.

The Quest of the Hero

Children should progressively develop a sense of the "one story" of all literature: the story of the loss and regaining of identity. This "story" is exemplified in the quest of the mythical hero whose adventures, death, disappearance, and return become the four generic plots of literature: romance, tragedy, irony-satire, and comedy.

Children should experience the hero stories in versions appropriate to their level of understanding. Younger children, for example, might be told aloud the story of David and Goliath; older students might be expected to read the same story themselves from the scriptures or a collection of Bible stories.

The hero stories of all cultures would be included in learning sequences, for variety and for the sake of comparison. Besides the hero tales of the Judaeo-Christian tradition, there are the Greek tales of Perseus, Theseus, and Hercules. There is the ancient epic of Gilgamesh, written in cuneiform five thousand years ago, that tells of a Sumerian king who undertook a long, dangerous journey in a search for immortality. There is the English epic of Beowulf and the tale of King Arthur, and the traditional French and German stories of Roland and Siegfried.

The concept of the quest of the hero offers numerous possibilities for critical analysis. A comparison of hero tales from many lands will reveal similarities in story form and structure: in most stories, for instance, a mystery surrounds the hero's birth. The *pattern* of the hero story will become evident to them as children read or listen to numbers of these tales. Comparison of the hero of the traditional tale with the hero or principal character of modern fiction is inevitable. Children may be led to an understanding of how all such stories, old and new, are alike in form and structure although their content may differ dramatically. Each story is in its way the story of a search for identity. Even in modern tales the young hero is likely to undergo a series of trials that often include a climactic adventure, and in many cases a kind of ritual death, a story pattern that reaches back to myth. In modern realistic fiction the hero has very different powers of action than has the hero of myth and romance; as they gain familiarity with all types of hero stories, children will be able to see these differences for themselves.

In reading and discussing the characteristics of the hero—ancient and modern—children may be led to an understanding of how the story of the hero's quest connects with the two opposite poles of man's imagination. The hero, as he works to restore a lost perfection or harmony or to gain recognition or identity, is very likely someone with whom we would like to identify; his enemies and the negative aspects of his environment, on the other hand, represent our fears and nightmares or what we would like to avoid.

Character Conventions

Children should begin to understand that certain types of characters are common to certain types of stories, that the same *type* of character keeps turning up in different forms in all kinds of stories.

Exposure to hero stories and discussion of the concept of the hero in fiction will be one way to illustrate the principle of recurrent character types. Typical character types other than the hero may be isolated for examination: the evil goddess of the myth is related to the witch of the romance, to the evil stepmother of the fairy tale, and to the impossible female parent as depicted in a number of modern ironic stories for children. The helpful goddess of myth becomes the kindly sorceress of romance, the fairy godmother of the fairy tale, and the kindly mother figure of the modern realistic story.

Children will be able to see what basic types of characters are associated with the hero's quest and which basic types are against it. They will note that there are neutral, flat, or static characters in many stories who add little to the action but who have other functions: to make the hero look more heroic, to make him appear more handsome, or more clever, to give him assistance, to be his "straight man."

Children should not be required to make moral judgments about the characters they encounter. They should be helped to see that characters of all kinds are needed as *structural principles* in story. In *The 500 Hats of Bartholomew Cubbins,* for instance, the role of villain is served by the Grand Duke Wilfred, nephew to the king, who is portrayed as sadistically cruel, haughty, and contemptuous. His characteristics are certainly not those that a conscientious teacher hopes young readers will emulate. However, it would be unfortunate to moralize about Wilfred's behavior in an effort to influence children not to behave as he does. Wilfred is central to the structure of the story. His sadistic interest in permanently getting rid of both Bartholomew *and* his hats leads the hero into dangerous and suspenseful situations that culminate in the climax of the story, where the duke is about to push Bartholomew from a parapet to his death. The fact that Bartholomew's adversaries now include a boy his own age, but his opposite in character and social status, provides by means of contrast and comparison an added dimension to the conflict. Not only does Wilfred move the plot forward, but his actions also move it into added excitement and suspense; rather than censuring his nastiness, readers should consider what the story would be like without the evil Wilfred, and gain more literary profit in the process.

Cyclical and Dialectical Imagery

Experience with both poetry and story, if the teacher structures learning sequences designed to foster insights, can lead the children to an understanding of the two structures that underlie literary imagery. The cyclical pattern is exemplified in the association of certain seasons and times of year with particular stories or parts of stories. Beginnings and quests, for instance, are likely to take place in the "merry months" of May and June, as in the old ballads. Endings and failures are often associated with the "death" of the year: fall and winter. Triumph, the full powers of the hero, and the like are most often associated with spring and summer.

A dialectical structure also underlies literary imagery. Man's dreams and visions are associated with gardens and paradises; his nightmares with deserts, threatening forests, and wastelands. As man seeks in his literature to identify with a neutral nature, he uses certain natural settings to reflect atmosphere and mood. Some colors are associated with dreams, others with nightmares. Black and grey are most often the colors of the sinister, for example; gold and white, of the noble and pure. (It may be pointed out that this has no relation whatsoever to race. It is probable that dark colors are sinister because the darkness of night terrified man; the gold of the sun warmed him.) The unicorn, lamb, and dove—peaceful animals and birds—are friends of the hero of romance, to use another example; but the serpent and the raven typically belong with the dark powers that oppose him.

As they read both poetry and story, children should be led toward an understanding of the kind of language employed in literature. The literary imagination has always sought to suggest an identity between the human mind and the world outside it. It does so by means of metaphor, the language of identification: "This is that." This process of identification or association, by means of words, began with early man's identification with animals, plants, and the forces of nature when he created stories that featured man-like gods who were associated with the sun, the sea, and other natural objects and phenomena. The process continues from mythology and is the very essence of literary expression.

Structuring Learning Sequences with Story

Though actual classroom discussion will seldom be as "perfect" as the simulated discussions given below, they are included to illustrate how the basic critical understandings just described may be fostered through careful questioning. The teacher may select specific stories for presentation that exemplify the particular understanding he wants to develop. However, children are encouraged, in the course of the discussion, to call upon *all* of their literary experiences where they apply to the subject under consideration.

I. Aim of the sequence: To lead children in the primary grades of elementary school toward an understanding that stories come in certain conventional "shapes."

Discussion:

Teacher: We have read *Little Tim and the Brave Sea Captain, Where the Wild Things Are,* and *The Tale of Peter Rabbit.* They are all stories about very different things, it's true, but can you think of any ways the stories are alike?

Pupils: —Tim and Peter and Max all do exciting things.
—They all get into danger.
—They leave home and go far away.
—And have great adventures.
—Lots of things happen to them.
—But they all get home okay at the end.
—Everything ends happy, except Peter feels sick.
—But he did okay; he got away from the man who was chasing him.
—Max didn't really go away; it was just a dream.
—It's the same thing, though. He went away in his mind.

Teacher: Could you say that the stories are shaped like this? *(He draws a circle on the board.)*

Pupils: —Yeah. They all end up where they started.
—Max goes away and has a trip and comes back to his room.
—Peter runs away from his house and gets into trouble in the garden and comes back home at the end.
—So does Tim.

Teacher: Do you know any other stories that have that same shape?

Pupils: —In "The Three Billy Goats Gruff" they don't come back to any place, but they end up safe at the end. Is that the same thing?
—Sure. It's the same way with lots of stories. Bad things

happen all the way through, but things turn out okay
at the end.
—That's the way it always is. Even in westerns. The good
guy ends up okay even though he nearly gets killed.
—I know one story where that doesn't happen: the Gingerbread Boy doesn't get away safe at the end. He gets
eaten.
—That doesn't happen very often in stories, though.
—Most of them are circles. They end up with things okay,
just the way they started.

II. Aim of the sequence: To help older children to the understanding that the hero story relates to the dialectical structure of
literary imagery. The hero's quest involves his effort to regain a
lost identity, to restore harmony or perfection.

Discussion:

Teacher: What does the hero most often do in these stories?
Pupils: —He goes looking for something, like Sir Lancelot looking
for the Holy Grail.
—Or Jason after the Golden Fleece.
—He goes to capture an enemy or get rid of something
horrible.
—Right. Perseus was trying to kill that monster Medusa.
—Sometimes he acts on a challenge or dare.
—Hercules had to do twelve labors as a punishment for
committing a murder.
—Sometimes the guy goes to do something because he's
really unhappy about the way things are where he is
and he wants to change them.
—I guess you could say Moses did that.
—Not only Moses. Superman does the same thing.
—Does that count? He's not one of these old heroes.
—He's still supposed to be a hero.
—Some heroes just go to seek their fortunes, like some
of those types in fairy tales. You're always getting
youngest sons who leave home to try and make it big.
—The hero is always looking for something good or for
something better. He seems to be looking for *something.*
—Something good. A hero story always has some kind
of search in it.

Teacher: Is that true of heroes and heroines in modern stories that we've read? Take *Call It Courage,* for an example.

Pupils: —Sure. That kid is searching for something. He's trying to find his own courage, I guess you could say.

—And the guy in *The Loner* is looking for something, too. I'm not sure exactly what or if he even knows at the beginning.

—Sure he does. He doesn't like the life he has to lead. He tries to find something better. It's still a search.

—They're all the same, these heroes. They have a dream that they want to make come true.

III. Aim of the sequence: To help older children gain an understanding of the cyclical structure that underlies literary imagery.

Discussion:

Teacher: If you were to write about something unpleasant or sad, what season of the year would you be likely to have it take place in?

Pupils: —Probably in the fall when things are dying.

—Or in the winter when they're dead.

Teacher: And if you were writing a happy story?

Pupils: —It could be in the winter, if you liked snow and stuff. Winter and fall.

—That's not the point. In most stories good things are put with good weather.

—I don't agree.

Teacher: Suppose we think of it in another way. *(Draws a circle on the chalkboard and labels each of its parts: summer, spring, fall, and winter, respectively.)* Let's see if this makes any sense according to the stories we know. First, what happens in the spring and summer in nature?

Pupils: —Things start growing.

—Everything is alive.

—Everything is green and new and fresh.

Teacher: What happens in fall and winter to natural things?

Pupils: —They die.

—Or go to sleep under the snow; seeds, I mean.

Teacher: Now, can you think of any stories you know that are spring stories, *even though they don't mention that time of year?*

Pupil: —You mean where stories are like the seasons, in a way.

Teacher: That's right.

Pupils: —Well, I guess you could say that "The Sleeping Beauty" begins as a winter story and ends as spring.

—So does "Beauty and the Beast."

—And "Cinderella."

—And "The Ugly Duckling!"

—And even *Charlie and the Chocolate Factory.*

—*Charlotte's Web,* too.

—Practically all stories for that matter go from bad to good at the end, sort of.

—Right! In *Charlotte's Web* they're all set to kill Wilbur at the beginning, but he's safe at the end.

—Most stories I've read or heard of are like that. They start out peaceful for a while, then everything gets scarey and dangerous, maybe, but it all ends up okay.

—So, it's something like a circle, like the seasons in a way, I guess: summer, fall, or winter, then spring again.

Teacher: There's another way we might look at this. We said that spring was a time when natural things were just beginning to grow, and summer when they have grown and developed. What stories do you know that are "spring" stories, where the hero is just beginning to grow?

Pupil: —You mean to get bigger?

Teacher: Well, partly, but it could also mean to grow up. What does it mean to grow up?

Pupils: —You start to learn things.

—Things happen to you to give you experiences you haven't had before. Is that what you mean?

Teacher: Yes. Are there any stories like that?

Pupils: —Sure. *Rufus M.* is one. Rufus is starting to grow up.

—Manolo in *Shadow of a Bull* grows up when he decides that he knows best about his own future.

—The guy in *The Flight of the Doves* grows up; he has to, to take care of his sister.

—Mafatu in *Call It Courage* grows up fast. He has to learn to take care of himself.

—It's the same with the boy in *Dorp Dead.*

—In most stories people learn things about people and what happens in life.

—And they learn about themselves. Mafatu learned that he really did have the courage to fight the sea.

Teacher: Could you say that those are seasonal stories?

Pupil: —You could compare them to the seasons, I guess; to spring and summer, maybe.

Teacher: This is harder: do you know any autumn or winter stories?

Pupils: —*The Jazz Man,* maybe. That's a sad story. The kid suffers a lot and things don't get much better for him at the end.

—The Norse myth we read, "The Death of Balder," is a winter story; Balder is dead at the end.

—But even there it says that he's going to a place after he dies where it's always summer.

—*Sounder* is an autumn and winter story, but even there you get the idea that there's some hope. Things won't always be so bad for the boy.

—Maybe. But even so at the end his family still has a pretty bleak future in a lot of ways.

—A wintry future!

IV. Aim of the sequence: To bring children toward an understanding of the dialectical structure that underlies patterns of literary imagery.

Discussion:

Teacher: Let's try out a game like "Twenty Questions" on some of the stories we know. The categories of the game are animal, vegetable, and mineral. Now suppose the story is a happy one, what animals would be likely to be associated with it?

Pupils: —I've never thought of it before, but I guess it would be gentle animals, you know, animals that are used to being with people, like the horse in *The Goose Girl.*

—Cats are usually on the good guy's side. Dick Whittington had a cat.

—Puss in Boots helped his master out.

—Pigs are often heroes themselves; like Padre Porko!

—Or Wilbur in *Charlotte's Web.*

—Wolves and foxes, things like that, are usually the "bad
guys," always playing tricks and trying to eat up the
hero.

—Like in "The Three Little Pigs."

—And "Little Red Riding Hood."

—And in "Henny Penny."

Teacher: All right. Now, think of the natural surroundings in
stories that tell about happy things. What kind of plants
are there in those, usually? What does the countryside
look like?

Pupils: —When everything's okay and things are going fine for
the hero, he's usually in a nice place, comfortable, like
his own house, maybe.

—But when he's in trouble, things usually look pretty
gloomy with lots of rocks and no trees.

—Like Perseus. The place where he was looking for Medusa was all grey with no sun ever shining there.

—And Rapunzel was banished to a dark wood and then
to a place like a desert.

—Yeah, but when the prince found her again, they went
to a neat palace where everything looked nice.

—Practically all stories are like that, I guess. Writers put
all the good things together.

—Things around you sort of match the way you feel.

—Well, anyway, they do in stories.

V. Aim of the sequence: To lead children to an awareness
of the dialectic structure that underlies literary imagery, man's
two dreams as expressed in his literature. At one limit of his desire
is the wasteland or wilderness; at the other is his vision of a garden
or paradise.

Discussion:

Teacher: Most people daydream, I think. I know a few people
right here who do. I do myself. What exactly is a daydream?

Pupils: —If you're bored, or mad, or something, you just think of a better place to be and go there in your mind.
—You make up something in your mind that takes you away from where you are. You take a trip!
—In your head.

Teacher: We talk about daydreams but not about day-night-mares. Why is that?

Pupil: —Most daydreams are about things you want or wish you could do; they're not about horrible things that you want to get away from. Nightmares are.

Teacher: Have you ever thought that stories show both kinds of dreams, pleasant dreams and nightmares?

Pupils: —Almost all stories are about making some dream or wish come true.
—People want a better life, maybe, and they try to make what they want happen.

Teacher: What stories do you know that are like that? Start by thinking of the myths and hero tales we have read.

Pupils: —Moses wanted to lead the children of Israel to where they wouldn't be slaves any longer.
—Prometheus wanted to give fire to man so he could live a better life, one more like the gods.
—Gilgamesh wanted to find a place where people were always young and there was no death.

Teacher: Are there any newer stories that show the same thing?

Pupils: —The biography of Harriet Tubman. She was leading slaves out of captivity, like Moses.
—Stories about pioneers show them working hard to make their surroundings more civilized and fit to live in. The *Little House* books tell all about that.
—In *Journey Outside* the boy is tired of his life with the Raft People who always talk about finding a better place to live but don't do anything about it. Dilar goes himself and finds something better. He wants his grandfather and the others to share it with him.

Teacher: Do people in books always succeed in making their dreams come true?

Pupils: —Not always. It's a sad story when they don't, though.
—But that's the way things are in real life. You can't

always get what you want. Too many stories are phoney. Somebody wants to get something or do something and no matter what, but it always works out okay at the end and he gets what he was after. In a lot of stories, like the ones on TV, you know beforehand that whatever the person wants he'll get. It's phoney.

—Maybe it is, but there wouldn't be any story if the person in it wasn't trying to get something or do something, would there?

—Well, he doesn't always have to get his own way. That's not the way things are in life.

—Right. But we're talking about stories, and most stories end up with *something* happening that the hero or whoever wanted to have happen at the beginning.

—Sometimes it's not exactly like making a dream come true, but things are better at the end than they were at the beginning. In *It's Like This, Cat,* the kid didn't have any big dreams come true, but at least at the end of the story he felt a little better about his family and everything.

—Right. You could say that dreams go in both directions: up and down!

Structuring Additional Learning Sequences

Classification and Categorization

It will help children become aware of recurrent structures and patterns and themes if they try to classify what they read in different ways. Many stories will fit into more than one category. Categories may be evolved with the children or supplied by the teacher. Stories may be classified in any of the following ways.

—According to the dialectic pattern: stories may show the world man wants and the world he rejects; often one story can handle the struggle between these two opposites. Some stories show the realization of the goals man seeks; others show his failure to "lift himself up," showing bitterness and defeat.

—According to the hero's power of action: whether it is greater than ours, less, or much the same. The categories might be provided for the children, with them working in groups to classify the stories they know. Comic and cartoon characters should be included: Superman is like a god, Charlie Brown is an ordinary chap, Dark Shadows is like a beast or demon.

—By their "shapes": comic, romantic, tragic, ironic. The characteristics of each story "shape" are elicited from the children after experience with all kinds of stories. Students can work in groups to list stories that show the cyclical nature of poetic imagery: "spring" stories are in the comic mode ("Beauty and the Beast"; *The Pushcart War; The Dragon Takes a Wife*); "summer" stories are in the romantic mode ("Mollie Whuppie"; *The Courage of Sarah Noble; Julie of the Wolves*); "fall" stories are in the tragic mode ("Death of Balder"; *John Henry; A Figure of Speech*); "winter" stories are in the ironic-satiric mode (*The Summer Birds; Tuck Everlasting; The Stonecutter*).

To help students understand satire and irony, have them collect examples from the following.

—Everyday speech: People often say, "That's great!" when they mean, "That's awful!" Why do people use words in this way? What would be the effect if we always said what we meant?
—Exaggerated stories: Tall tales, fish stories, and so forth.
—Verbal insults: "Did your mother have any children?"
—Jingles and rhymes: "Sing a song of sixpence," "Peter, Peter, Pumpkin Eater," "Hey, Diddle, Diddle."
—Songs of nonsense, fantasy and satire: "Yankee Doodle," "Oh, Susanna," "Sucking Cider Through a Straw."
—Limericks and tongue twisters: Examples should be presented orally.

A follow-up might be a discussion of advertisements. By using archetypal, idealized images, advertisements make a forceful appeal. Does anyone believe it when they're told that "This is the best movie of the decade; not to be missed?" How literally do people take claims that face creams will transform complexions overnight, or that certain floor cleaners will make an old floor like new?

Most children's stories are written in the romantic or comic modes, but there are some with ironic twists; these are the stories that do not end in wish-fulfillment or those that expose follies (*Nobody's Family's Going to Change,* "The Emperor's New Clothes").

Stories may be classified in a number of other ways, the sophistication of the classifications varying in accordance with the ability of grades and classes within grades:

> —Stories that end happily or sadly
> —Stories of successful quests
> —Stories of wish-fulfillment
> —Stories of dreams and stories of nightmares

The categories are supplied by the teacher as well as by a number of the stories, but the examples are drawn from all aspects of the children's literary and sub-literary experience. They will find, for instance, examples of the wish-fulfillment story not only in classic tales like "Cinderella," but also in many television commercials and serials as well as films.

The following activities can help children to learn to classify stories.

—Play a game similar to "Twenty Questions" with literary imagery. For example, in the story "The Death of Balder," *animal imagery* is represented by hounds of prey; the *vegetable world* is a wilderness; in *mineral imagery* there are rocky glens.
—Create charts to show the *symbolic association of color* with people's dreams and desires and with what they reject: white is used to portray purity and innocence; in the western, the bad guys wear black. However, one color may have more than one association: in one context red, for example, may signify courage; in another, revolt.
—Make a collage of titles that show the *quest myth*. Find examples from all types of children's literature: myth, legend, folk and fairy tale, fantasy, realism, historical fiction, biography. Find examples from comics, movies, television, even actual life.
—Collect examples of *archetypes* from television, comics, advertis-

ing, and films. Examples: the detergent that fights dirt as the knight fights the dragon; images of paradise in soft drink commercials; cars that are cougars and rabbits; hand cream that magically transforms chapped hands; the "Cinderella" story: the young man can't get a date until the right mouthwash "saves" him, etc.

Other Learning Activities

Reading and listening to stories, asking questions and offering ideas in guided discussion will form the greatest part of criticism for elementary and middle school students. Long writing assignments and those without adequate prewriting discussions should be avoided. To help children consolidate literary understandings, the following types of activities, involving art, discussion, composition, drama, or a combination of these techniques, are useful.

Art

—Children at all levels can be helped to see that stories have form through their own attempts at drawing the shape of a story (see figure 7.1).
—Picture essays can be developed showing images of desirable and undesirable worlds: straight roads or paths and mazes, trees in bloom and rows of telephone poles, domesticated animals and beasts of prey or monsters, homes and prisons, gardens and wastelands, productive people and derelicts, gentle waterfalls and destructive floods, human compassion and human cruelty.
—Students create "Me" collages using magazine pictures. They find images from the animal, vegetable, and mineral worlds that they

FIGURE 7.1.   Drawing the Shape of a Story

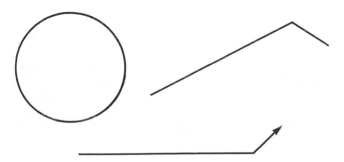

identify themselves with: dog, whale, elephant, mouse; artichoke, tomato, turnip, lily, tree; jewel, rock, piece of plastic, razor. Crests may be made to adorn the collages, showing pictorially the meaning of the students' names (Sally Smith uses a picture of a blacksmith for her crest) and using the color they identify with. A variation on this exercise is to divide the collage into two parts: "Me" and "Not Me." The opposing images show what the person rejects or does not identify with.

Art and Composition

—Make picture essays to show how people attempt to identify, in their naming and design, made objects and human activities with nature. (Automobiles are named for animals; fashions make use of fur, feathers, flowers, and floral patterns; in hairstyles we have pony tails, poodle cuts, and beehives.)
—Imaginations can create in words or with words and pictures: (a) A city in the year 3000: Where is it? How does it look? What do the inhabitants look like? What do they do at work? At play? What type of transportation do they use? (b) A utopia: Where would an ideal world or community be located? How do the people get work done? What are their values? How have they handled the problems that keep our world from being utopian?

Debate

—For a debate: Resolved: "There are no heroes in modern life." Questions to consider in the debate: If there are modern heroes, who are they? What is the definition of a hero? Has this definition changed over time? Can anyone be a hero? How is it possible for one to be the hero of one's own life? And so on.

Discussion

—Panel discussions of various kinds are possible even when panelists have read different books. General literary questions applicable to novels of the same type, say contemporary realism, may be discussed as early as fourth grade. With the children helping to frame them, questions are posed for the panelists: What was the problem or undesirable situation (conflict) faced by the main character(s) in the story? How was it solved? (by magical means, through coincidence, by effort on the part of the characters themselves?) How story problems are solved in contemporary realistic novels may be compared and contrasted with how they are solved in myth, legend, and folk and fairy tale. (In the old tales often the hero has magical powers or help from a divine being directly or in the form of a magic talisman, such as a cloak of darkness, sword or shield, and so forth.)

Examination of modern popular fantasies such as *Star Wars* and those featuring James Bond shows that these latter-day heroes have much in common with the heroes of traditional literature. (Many of James Bond's elaborate technological devices are magical in effect; Luke Skywalker has "The Force" with him, and Yoda, one of the wise old men found throughout literature, is his teacher and adviser.)

Discussions like these show how archetypes (certain characters, symbols, story types, etc.) are recurrent in literature and illustrate that, depending on the type of story they are in, heroes have different degrees of power. (In myth, legend, and many fairy tales their powers are magical; in fantasy they are larger than life, often with magic to help them; in modern realistic stories heroes and heroines are ordinary people.)

Middle graders can make comparisons based on a particular type of literature such as the folktale, reading examples from different cultures and perhaps noting motifs that are common to all or appear only in some. (Like archetypes, but having less universality, *motifs* are images, symbols, and the like that recur in individual stories or certain types of stories.) Motifs may be characters like the noodle-head who appears in one type of folktale, of which "Epaminondes" is a good example; the witch; the wise old man; the disguised individual; the wicked stepmother, to name a few. The magical talisman, spells, curses, and wishes are also motifs. Noting these in the folktales of many cultures helps students see how literary works are related and connected.

Examination of traditional literature is especially useful in discovering how story works, since these early tales are, in effect, blueprints for stories that follow them. In them literary conventions are easy to see: characters and events appearing in groups of three (three trials, three attempts at rescue, three wishes); the happy ending culminating often in a marriage feast; the triumph of good over evil no matter what the odds.

Panelists might discuss specific examples from contemporary literature, television, movies, or comics of recurrent motifs and conventions. After discussion, these might be collected and pictorially represented in a mural in which one side shows how the motifs or conventions are used in folktales and the other how they are still used in contemporary stories. Interestingly, motifs and conventions common to a particular type of story are easy to spot in the formula stories common to television: in police shows there are often three tries to catch the killer; situation comedies are filled with stock characters (henpecked husbands, tough guys, buffoons); in countless stories good triumphs over evil, if only in the last few seconds of a show.

—Create for mature students or have them create detailed story-kits. Brainstorm to develop the characteristics of a hero or heroine: physical, mental, emotional, social; be specific. Set the qualities down on a chart with columns for the various character traits. (Compare this exercise with the development of a character in the popular game "Dungeons and Dragons," which older pupils may know.) Given the characters' traits, place them in a setting (time, place). Characters with magical powers will require remote settings, as in legend and fantasy; characters with ordinary or extraordinary human powers may operate in realistic, everyday settings.

Pose a problem for the character to solve: kill a monster that is destroying the animals of the community, find a lost child, set out to discover why the spring has not come back, etc. Through discussion, work out how the character will react and why, in various episodes that lead to the resolution of the problem.

Although someone may eventually write out the story, it is more important to spend plenty of time in oral discussion to work it out in every detail. Set story problems for small groups within the class to solve, then share the solutions.

Discussion and Composition

—Transformation or *metamorphosis* is a common literary archetype, probably because it has deep appeal to the human imagination. In ancient stories and in some contemporary fantasy, actual physical transformations take place; in realistic modern stories change occurs more subtly as a change in character. Have students watch television commercials and magazine advertisements for examples of metamorphosis created by the modern imagination. What is transformed? (Bad breath becomes sweet.) What magic agent effects the transformation? (The hero, Mouthwash.) What are the rewards? (Success in love or in a job.)

In a follow-up activity, students might enjoy creating their own advertisements, using the archetype of metamorphosis.

—Write cooperatively an original mythology. Brainstorm ideas in small groups and with the whole class. The mythology is for an imaginary group of people of whom the students are members. This group lived centuries ago or will live in the future on another planet. List the things that would most concern these people: What sort of place do they live in? What hardships, if any, must they endure from their physical surroundings? What is their greatest need? What frightens them? Why are they in that place? Where did they come from? What kind of society do they want to build? Let students slowly, over time, work out the mythology, using brief notes. To assign writing too soon makes the assignment seem difficult and overwhelming. (It will be interesting to see whether the created mythology will work in a "circle": the group once knew a golden age or perfect time, lost it, and seeks to recover it.)

—Plan a short film or cartoon story that uses the rhythm of the seasons to tell a human story. (The film need not be shot; planning a series of shots is a satisfying group activity. Planning is done on a *storyboard,* using a series of sketches that show the sequence of shots and whether they are close-ups, medium-range, or long shots.) Example:

Frame 1: Long shot of an autumn scene: dark sky, leafless trees

Frame 2: Close-up of a leaf falling from a tree

Frame 3: Long shot of a family group at a railroad station

Frame 4: Close-up of tearful faces

Frame 5: Medium shot of father boarding the train alone

Drama

—Groups might dramatize, through mime, interesting metaphors from their reading. As in charades, a team acts out the metaphor while the others guess what it is.

—To a drumbeat, students mime changes (transformations): "You are holding something very hot; as the beat slows, the object changes into a small, pointed object; as the beat quickens, it becomes a small living thing like a bird or butterfly that escapes or is set free."

Using movement and sound, students transform themselves imaginatively in quick succession into three different objects: a baby, a fluttering leaf, a rock.

Once a teacher understands that all literature is linked together by means of common elements that recur continually, it will be easy to think of ways to help children see connections among their literary, personal, and cultural lives. The character types, events, stories, images, and themes that appear and reappear in literature are present in music, art, television, movies, games, current events, advertising, comics, and cartoons. Discovering these elements and making connections among them gives an added dimension to the enjoyment of individual poems and stories. Literature adds up to an exciting whole. Its influence is recognized as widespread and timeless. Man's imaginative expressions are as old as the first story and as new as each young critic's imaginative response to it.

Teaching structural principles is teaching how literature works and what it is. It is not only separate works that may be admired or despised but a unified imaginative structure of archetypal themes, conventional images and forms. There is intellectual excitement in discovering what literature is and increased imaginative power in the discovery.

Chapter 8

Composing Poetry
and Story

Young people should certainly be encouraged to write,
for everyone can learn to write poetry up to a point—the
point of discovering how difficult it is to write it unusually
well. To get to that point is no mean achievement, as
it is well past the substandard level of naive or doggerel
verse which is the usual mode of amateur expression. But
the purpose of such encouragement is to breed a love of
poetry, not to breed poets.

NORTHROP FRYE*

Poetic Composition: An Aspect of
the Critical Process

Literature grows out of other literature, and experience with
poetry is the best way to foster its creation. The children in the
elementary school should hear poetry in quantity, they should
speak it themselves, ask questions of each other and the teacher,
compare and contrast different kinds and types of poems and poetic
techniques, and they should in freedom be allowed to experiment
with poetic creations of their own.

The poet Kenneth Koch, acting on the assumption that children
are natural poets, went into a number of classrooms to teach children that they could make poems out of the expression of their
"wishes, lies, and dreams." He found it most important to take "children seriously as poets. Children have a natural talent for writing

*"Poetry," *University of Toronto Quarterly*, vol. xxvi (April 1956), p. 290.

poetry and anyone who teaches them should know that. Teaching really is not the right word for what takes place: it is more like permitting the children to discover something they already have."*

When education for literacy is begun by developing and releasing "something they already have," children are likely to respond with the energy, enthusiasm, and creativity that Koch describes in his book. Since poetry is a part of their natural expression, the use of it is essential in an education that aims to develop literacy.

Input for Writing: Exposure to Forms

Writing according to a form is both a discipline and a freedom. The young poet is helped in his composition if he is provided with a pattern, as Kenneth Koch demonstrated when he had his young fellow-poets create according to formulae, either suggested by him or evolved by the children in collaboration with him. There are numerous forms that provide simple enough patterns for the expression of the children's own thoughts, experiences, wishes, dreams, and desires.

Of course, the hasty reading of one or two examples does not prepare children to write in a given form. To give children in-school experience with poetry requires planning and preparation. For whatever reasons, poetry is a neglected art both in and out of school. Researcher Chow Hoy Tom found that most teachers did not read poetry aloud regularly.† Ann Terry, who researched children's poetry preferences, found that they enjoy narrative and humorous poems and those with strong patterns of rhythm and rhyme.‡ Lack of experience with poetry undoubtedly limits children's preferences.

A good way to become familiar with the wide range of excellent children's poetry available today is a series of browsing sessions in the library. It is useful to have an anthology of personal favorites, and this is how to begin to compile it. In selecting fine contemporary verse, a place to begin is with the winners of the National Council of Teachers of English Award for Excellence in Poetry for Children. Each poet has published several volumes. The first recipient, in 1977, was David McCord, followed by Aileen Fisher (1978), Karla Kuskin (1979), Myra Cohn Livingston (1980), Eve Merriam (1981), and John Ciardi (1982).

*Kenneth Koch, *Wishes, Lies and Dreams* (New York: Chelsea House, 1970), p. 25.
†Chow Hoy Tom, "Paul Revere Rides Ahead: Poems Teachers Read to Pupils in the Middle Grades," *Library Quarterly*, vol. xliii (January 1972), pp. 27–38.
‡Ann Terry, *Children's Poetry Preferences* (Urbana, Ill.: National Council of Teachers of English, 1974).

Riddles and Conundrums

The puns and word play of riddles are not only close to the mental processes of children, they are also an effective and palatable way to "teach" simile and metaphor. In riddles, things are described in terms of other things. The French poet Mallarmé's prescription for writing *poetry* was to describe not the thing but the effect it produces. Riddles would seem to be an excellent way to let a child's own metaphorical processes serve as an introduction to poetry.

We have already discussed how experience with these forms can lead naturally into the creation of original riddles, even with the very young. First lines for original works may be supplied by the teacher or contributed by class members. It may be profitable to work out one or two examples as a cooperative effort, the inspired sparking the uninspired. The creation of original riddles will help the child to see ordinary objects in new ways and to create fresh metaphors to describe them, an essential aspect of the poetic experience.

Unrhymed Forms

Rhythmic repetitions. The child's natural propensity for repetitive patterns should be indulged. The vivid images of Hilda Conkling's "I Am" might serve as a pattern for original verse:

> I am willowy boughs
> For coolness;
> I am gold-finch wings
> For darkness;
> I am a little grape
> Thinking of September
> I am a very small violet
> Thinking of May.

For older children the sonorous repetitive rhythms of the Bible might supply a pattern:

> PSALM 150
>
> Praise ye the Lord.
> Praise God in his sanctuary:
> Praise him in the firmament of his power.

Praise him for his mighty acts:
Praise him according to his excellent greatness.
Praise him with the sound of the trumpet:
Praise him with the psaltery and harp.
Praise him with the timbrel and dance:
Praise him with stringed instruments and organs.
Praise him upon the loud cymbals:
Praise him upon the high sounding cymbals.
Let everything that has breath praise the Lord.
Praise ye the Lord.

Catalogue verse. Catalogue verse is as old as Homer. Vivid imagery, the basic stuff of poetry, is the heart of catalogue verse. There is no need to struggle for rhyme. An entire class may participate, the younger children dictating their ideas on a common subject while the teacher transcribes, arranging the lines in different lengths for maximum rhythmic appeal. After priming minds with a poem or two read aloud, the teacher mentions a favorite theme and the children, in a brainstorming session, call out their associations related to it, trying to express as many sensory reactions as possible. The theme might be the school itself; the poem grows with items like these: "the whirr of the pencil sharpener," "the woolly smell of damp coats drying on a winter afternoon," "songs off-key," "dusty taste of chewed pencils."

Older children working in small groups or individually create their own expressive word pictures. Rupert Brook's "The Great Lover" was the stimulus material for these lines:

These I have loved:
    Sunlight on a silken cat's back
    Clear June days
    White sails like birds in flight over the bay
    Green trees flecked with bits of blossom
    And the icy touch of water as I dive.

The biblical litany uses parallel arrangements of words and ideas in poetic patterns, the arrangement of the lines providing a rhythmic sweep when the whole is read aloud. A holiday or a holy day could be the stimulation for such a poem, the teacher supplying the starting phrase, the children the rest, the whole transcribed for maximum rhythmic flow:

Let us always be thankful
   for

      _____

      _____

      _____

      _____

  for

      _____

      _____

      _____

Haiku and tanka. An ancient Japanese form of poetry is the haiku, which, in effect, is an image created within a set form of 17 syllables. A means of expressing deep emotion, it evokes more than it states: a haiku is a miniature lyric. Older children may delight in the discipline of strict adherence to the syllabic structure, but such adherence is not the important thing. More important is the expression of an idea or feeling, caught and recorded with vividness and precision:

     Hovering over us
     The sky surrounds the world
     Invented by God.

The tanka is the same as the haiku, with the addition of two seven-syllable lines at the end. It offers the means, for some children, of developing a thought more fully than they are able to do in the haiku, which is in essence a moment captured.

Cinquain. The cinquain also deals in pure imagery. It is an arrangement of five lines of two, four, six, eight, and two syllables, respectively. Line 1 states the title, line 2 describes the title, line 3 expresses an action, line 4 expresses a feeling, and line 5 gives another word or words for the title.

Rhymed Forms

Limericks. Nonsense verse is a particular delight for children and may be profitably used to reintroduce the joys of verse to older children who are skeptical of poetry or disenchanted as a result of negative experiences with it. Children enjoy the bounce and speed of the limerick, recognizing with smiles its suitability to humorous subjects, and easily following its rhythmic pattern by tapping it out. There are many thousands of excellent examples, like this particularly playful one by Edward Lear:

> There was an old person of Ware,
> Who rode on the back of a bear:
> When they asked, "Does it trot?" he said
> "Certainly not!
> He's a Moppsikon, Floppsikon bear!"

Couplets, tercets, and quatrains. Rhyme is an aspect of poetry that should not be stressed in children's writing of poetry. The creation of telling, vivid, fresh images is a more poetic endeavor. But children are intrigued by rhyme, and many of the poems written for them are rhymed. Reading couplets aloud and letting children supply the rhyming word is enjoyable ear training, for example:

> The world is so full of a number of things,
> I'm sure we should all be as happy as ———.

Supplying a first line and asking for a second is often a fruitful way to get young poets started.

Tercets are three-line units that may rhyme in two lines or all three, for example:

THE PEOPLE

> The ants are walking under the ground,
> And the pigeons are flying over the steeple,
> And in between are the people.

> *Elizabeth Madox Roberts*

Quatrains are four-line stanzas with a possibility of a number of rhyme schemes: aabb, abab, abcb. The rhythm of the quatrain is easy to tap out for it is regular and even:

THE TOASTER

> A silver-scaled Dragon with jaws flaming red
> Sits at my elbow and toasts my bread.
> I hand him fat slices, and then, one by one,
> He hands them back when he sees they are done.

> *William Jay Smith*

The class or a group within it may choose a common subject for their couplets, tercets, and quatrains, putting them all together at the end to make one long poem. Common topics may be descriptions of classmates, each person's impression of a common experience, or each individual effort an expression of a wish or hope.

Ballads. Ballads, particularly the old ones, employ a cinematic technique, the pictures flashing into the reader's mind as a result of the action described; ballads contain little exposition. But there is springy rhythm and rhyme, and often a refrain, as in "Robin Hood Rescuing the Widow's Three Sons":

> Now Robin Hood is to Nottingham gone,
> With a link and a down, and a day.
> And there he met a silly old woman,
> Was weeping on the way.

A story they have read, an incident from current events or history might serve as a topic for classroom balladeers working with partners or in small groups. The ballad pattern and its variations should be firmly in mind before composing begins as a result of considerable exposure to it by ear, for younger students; by ear and eye for those who can read independently.

Literary ballads and story-poems like those of Alfred Noyes are often imagistic and vividly descriptive as well as rhythmic and repetitive. Some of these will be included with the old ballads because they are effective and for purposes of comparison. Folk songs, sea chanties, work songs, cowboy songs, spirituals, and the like are similar to the old ballads in that they express the lore of the common folk. The use of all such forms provides numerous opportunities for writing: new words for old tunes, modern work songs set to the rhythms of the old, original lullabies that follow an old form, personal or group experiences ordered in the story form of the old ballad.

"Prose" into "Poetry"

Since the young child does not speak prose and is likely to write it haltingly and inaccurately, if at all, the teacher, confronted with his garbled manuscript, is likely to despair. Major surgery is required to turn what he finds there into acceptable prose. Suppose, however, when confronted with a jumbled paragraph about a pet, he restrains the correcting pencil and, instead, transcribes this:

> my dog my dog is. black with white. One black paw, the others white my dog is noisyHe barks a lot and he wags a lot. And he eats a lot. My dog is My Best Friend. We Run. We play and we have fun.

into this:

> My Dog
> My dog is
> Black with white
> One black paw
> The others white,
> My dog is
> Noisy
> He barks
> A lot
> He wags
> A lot
> He eats
> A lot.
> My dog is
> My Best Friend
> We run
> We play
> We have fun!

An imaginative and sympathetic treatment transforms what is in prose unnecessary repetition into an element of poetry, respects the child's natural expression, and offers him the encouragement needed to undertake more ambitious literary endeavors.

Poetic patterns may also be created by the alert teacher from the children's conversation, these "poems" used both as classroom reading material and as illustrations of how words may be ordered in poetic patterns. Such experiments will offer proof to the teacher of the children's natural propensity for repetition and the rhythmic use of language in their natural expression. A teacher, for example, might join a small group of kindergartners or first graders to share their talk about a recent visit to the zoo. Transcribed on his note pad or on an experience chart, their conversation might look like this:

> *Teacher:* What did you see at the zoo?
> *Pupils:* A lion, a lion, I saw a lion.
> Monkeys, I saw monkeys, lots of monkeys.
> I saw a tiny, tiny elephant.
> I saw a big baboon.
> A *big* baboon!
> At the zoo . . . at the zoo I saw a hippo,
> A huge old hippo.
> At the zoo . . .

Composing involves an ordering of experience in words. The emphasis is upon experimentation with all of the forms that poets have used to order experience. Composition may be oral or written but the children's literary efforts are always undertaken in the context of other literature, for literature is *created* out of other literature.

Composing Story: Part of the Process of Literary Criticism

Composing is an important aspect of the critical experience. A knowledge of form and structure of story comes firsthand from the attempt to write a story, particularly if the student tries to match the *structure* of a myth or fairy tale, perhaps using realistic incidents from his own time. Writing should come after exposure to forms, for literature grows out of literature itself, and children should not be expected to compose in a vacuum. Story can be created in movements, shapes, and color, as well as in words. It may be composed of the images that make up a film.

Literary Forms Order Experience

The composition of original stories should, of course, be an integral part of the curriculum in literary studies. Children in the elementary school should write story more than discursive prose, for it is through story that the child orders his experience and orients himself to the world. Children, as James Moffett says, "do all of their serious business in a play form. That is to say, it is a great mistake to regard their addiction to stories as mere childish pleasure seeking to be catered to until they have sobered up enough to reflect on life. They are already reflecting an enormous amount; we can't *stop* them from doing it. All adults have to do is recognize the function of their fun, and honor stories as a genuine mode of thought."* In *From Two to Five*, Chukovsky describes children who, deprived of fairy tales and fantasy, spontaneously spin their own as their method of coming to terms with the world.

Exposure to Literary Forms as Stimulus for Composition

Children may be helped toward precision and order in their process of ordering the world through language without loss of creativity and spontaneity. The selection and shaping that language involves, the choices between alternative expressions so that language will fit experience and give it life—these activities imply imaginative work. The teacher must be wise enough to find ways to channel verbal energy without binding it. Writing or composing orally on tape or dictating must be stimulated, nurtured, and guided with sympathy, tact, and a sense of purpose. Poetic patterns have been shown as necessary input in the process of freeing children to create their own poetry; story patterns have the same function. Providing the child with a pattern to give shape to his imaginings saves him hours of frustration; his creativity is aided rather than curtailed. Creation is facilitated by the use of technical conventions outside the individual that control his creative composition without suppressing it.

Inventing stories seems to be more difficult for a child than creating with paint or modeling materials, particularly if the child is asked to *write* a story. His vocabulary may be too limited to express his feelings, he may be held back by his lack of speed and skill in handwriting, his inhibitions about spelling, or his basic bewilderment about how to proceed. All too often children are told to write a story without sufficient prior motivation or stimulation in the form of models and materials. This is not to say that children should be taught to copy or that they should be in competition with

---

*James Moffett, *A Student-Centered Language Arts Curriculum, K-6: A Handbook for Teachers* (Boston: Houghton Mifflin, 1968), p. 118.

the professional and intimidated by him. Criticism that emphasizes literary form and structure as the means of shaping and ordering the imaginings of all writers, experienced or inexperienced, will help the young writer to see that he shares with all storytellers the same problems of composition and can only benefit from a consideration of their ways of dealing with these problems as he goes about setting down what necessarily must be his own personal interpretations of experience.

Impersonal forms provide structures into which children can project feeling unself-consciously. David Holbrook, the British educator who has had considerable success in freeing the most resistant children to write, favors the use of forms to release ideas and feelings.

> I felt the only way to achieve . . . expression was by using stimulant poems, passages, and themes which the child already recognized as means to the depersonalizing of his individual emotion—a way to that "third ground" which is a meeting-place between the "mind" of a community and his own. Such a depersonalized world, I have tried to suggest, exists in the sea-shanty, the folksong and the game rhyme. It also exists in such poetry as the Chinese poems translated by Arthur Waley. The fairy tale provides it, and so too, I think, do certain other conventional types of child's story— the story of exploration, for instance. And, it seems to me, that even the Wild Western may provide a half-serious, half-irresponsible world where self-identification may be indulged in.*

Children, in fact, turn naturally to literary forms and patterns they have encountered when they create stories of their own. Two psychologists conducted an extensive study in which they collected examples of the stories children tell and write. In *Children Tell Stories*, a book based on these studies, they reported that the imagined happenings from stories and pictures children had seen and heard figured largely in their representations of ordinary living. They created variants of fables and fairy tales, long adventure stories, and stories of ghosts and goblins. The children's stories, in their structure and use of symbol and imagery, showed striking similarities to literary archetypes: "of consuming oneself, of humor arising from incongruity and exaggeration, . . . of death and com-

*David Holbrook, *English for Maturity*, 2nd ed. (New York: Cambridge University Press, 1967), p. 115.

ing alive again . . . human relationships and hostile wishes and death."*

There must, then, be input before there can be output on the part of the child writer. Impressions and experiences may be unique but they require a convention for their expression in words.

Ideas of what originality is are often highly exaggerated; the best writers have always used the forms and conventions, even the ideas of those who came before, bringing their own individuality to their works. The child writer should be encouraged to do the same. He might rewrite a story using a different form, a myth as a story poem, say, or an adventure story as a play. He might write tales or story poems with contemporary settings that follow the pattern of old tales and ballads; the triad pattern of the fairy tales might be the form of a modern "realistic" story; the Cinderella story may be set down in modern terms; the hero's quest is not limited to ancient tales of romance and adventure, but may feature a youthful hero or heroine very like its young author; original tall tales may be created with the old ones as patterns; or young writers may create their own myths of origin along the lines of the myths of the primitives or by using the formula of Kipling's "just-so" stories.

Cooperative Composition

Group writing, like group discussion, should be encouraged. Compositions may be collective or individual in the group situation. The transition from collective to individual is likely to occur naturally as groups think up variations on a common theme, using each other's ideas as stimuli.

In a classroom with a healthy climate of encouragement and support, children gain much by reading each other's work, offering suggestions, giving each other help with word choice, spelling, and punctuation. Oral reading of one's own material gives it life and meaning that may be misinterpreted when a reader is confronted with a written form that falls short of presenting precisely what the youthful author meant to say. His own voice adds the inflections and intonations that his pen was too inexperienced to provide. Moreover, flaws in design are detected more readily when material is read aloud.

The children should be allowed to work as long as they need

*Evelyn Goodenough Pitcher and Ernst Prelinger, *Children Tell Stories: An Analysis of Fantasy* (New York: International Universities Press, 1963), pp. 8-9.

to on their rough drafts: revising, refurbishing, revamping. The teacher circulates, offering assistance to groups and individuals when it is asked for or when he recognizes the need. If the children are fully stimulated and prepared to write, and allowed to work cooperatively, frustrated pencil-chewing will give way more readily to eager pencil-pushing.

When putting words down on paper presents difficulties for young children, they should be encouraged to compose their stories orally, dictating them to an older student or to the teacher, or recording them on a tape that they can listen to, edit, and revise.

The "writer's workshop" in the classroom is preferable to lonely literary endeavors that are the result of homework assignments. The young writer requires aid and encouragement, both from his peers and his teacher, and this is forthcoming if he works at his compositions in a classroom climate of acceptance and sympathy for his efforts.

Case Histories in Composition

One fourth-grade class had read, in poetry and prose, the exploits of Robin Hood until they knew him and each of his merry men as old friends. In groups they set out to write their own episodes of the Robin Hood story, showing him and his men engaged in new adventures. Interest was high and the project continued for many days, resulting in a mimeographed booklet of some never-before recorded adventures of Robin Hood that would have delighted Howard Pyle as much as it did its authors.

A sixth-grade class concentrated on the short story. The teacher read aloud to them a wide selection of different types of stories: Poe's "The Tell-Tale Heart," O. Henry's "The Ransom of Red Chief," Saroyan's "Locomotive 88," Quentin Reynold's "A Secret for Two," Ray Bradbury's "Fever Dream," Ellis Parker Butler's "Pigs Is Pigs," and many more. The children themselves found others that they enjoyed in searches through library anthologies, prepared them, and read them aloud to the class. In addition, they listened to recordings of short stories read by professionals.

Together, working in groups, the children evolved a description of short story technique: few characters, economy of expression, early establishment of setting and situation, and so on. They then discussed possible subjects for short stories, with many students working out character sketches, settings, outlines of plots, and situations cooperatively. The writing took place in class. The important first paragraphs were tested on others and revised again and again to suit the requirements of the pupil-critics who were now in command of much that constitutes effective short story technique. Final dog-eared drafts were polished and read aloud; then last corrections were made. Proofreading was an important part of the project: the work had to be technically correct, since it was to be published for distribution among other classes and among parents. A bound copy, complete with card, was placed with the library's collection of short stories for circulation.

A fourth grade had read many myths of origin, particularly those found in the mythology of North American Indians: "Why the Robin Has a Red Breast," "How the Rabbit Got His Short Tail," and many others. Then they composed their own, dictating into a tape recorder marvelous explanations of why the grass is green, why the sky is blue, why dogs bark, and why birds sing.

A third grade delighted in the teacher's reading of the tall tales that tell of the exploits of Paul Bunyan and Pecos Bill. Then they wrote some taller tales of their own.

First graders composed tiny tales in the manner of nursery tales like "The Three Billy Goats Gruff" and "The Three Pigs," using children like themselves as their chief characters and fierce dogs, threatening witches, and snakes as their antagonists.

Mechanical Skills

The problem of honing and polishing mechanical skills is minimized when children work cooperatively, with excitement, on something they really want to do. Not every literary form encountered will provide the necessary stimulus for a class project, of course, and it is not advisable that it should. Some types of stories will enthrall and absorb more than others, and these will be the ones the children will most want to try themselves.

No author writes well, particularly as to the mechanics of writing, unless he has an audience. When the children write for each other, the audience is ready-made. If they know that others are interested in their ideas, they will work to perfect the skills necessary for effective communication. Certainly they will write more eagerly if they know their work will be shared by sympathetic readers and not merely found fault with by the red pencil. When composition comes first, handwriting, punctuation, spelling, and the like are put in their place—one of importance in facilitating communication, but always as part of an editing process, coming after having something to say and someone to say it to. Working with small groups and individuals, the teacher gives help with mechanical skills where it is needed. In every class there is such a wide range of ability in the use of language that it is a fruitless, yawn-inspiring endeavor to drill mechanical skills, the use of commas and capitals, spelling, and the like, to an entire class at once. More can be accomplished and more quickly with a few or with one pupil at a time. The child can read aloud from his imperfect prose and the teacher can show him how, with punctuation and the like, to give his words voice, and influence the poor speller to admit that, if he wants readers to share his ideas, he must use more familiar spellings.

The practice of having children write and "hand in" a composition for the teacher to grade is of dubious value as a learning experience. Confronted with a page of prose that seems to require nothing less than major surgery, it is the rare teacher who can refrain from the use of the correcting pencil. The child's next attempt at writing, if he makes one, is likely to repeat the same errors or show signs of inhibition as the author retreats into terse or insipid means of expression in an effort to minimize his errors and reduce the amount of red that will appear on his paper. When teachers do read the children's offerings, it will be more fruitful for all concerned if, as they read, they jot down notes for their own use in planning individual and small group lessons in areas that require improvement. One child may need help in constructing complete sentences or in subordinating ideas; another may have personal problems in spelling and usage that warrant special instruction; there may be indications in the work of several children that they would profit from special assistance in using words more precisely or in developing general ideas with elaborative detail. Occasionally the teacher will note a problem so widespread that it warrants a lesson for the entire class.

If the teacher does write a comment on a child's work, it should be a reaction to the ideas that he finds there, to indicate that the writer has communicated something of his experience, feelings, hopes, interests, wishes, or whatever he has tried to express. If, for example, a young writer has tried, in halting prose, to describe his delight in a new pet, the teacher's comment will show that he has "read" him if it goes something like this: "Your new cat sounds a lot like mine. I'd like to hear more about him!" Work with the student writer on the mechanics of his written expression will not be ignored but deferred. It can take place in a personal conversation, and what the writer has tried to communicate should take precedence over his mechanical problems of communication.

Another questionable practice for classroom composition is teacher acceptance of random outpourings for their own sake or for the sake of "self-expression." The therapeutic value of such excesses has not been proven, and, although the teacher may pride himself on accepting without question whatever the child writes, he is not helping him to grow in effectual use of language, a developmental growth that requires shaping, molding, guiding, and instructing.

Publication

Some children may prefer, for a number of reasons, not to share their literary efforts, even with the teacher, or at least not until he has proven himself a sympathetic audience. But most children will delight in seeing their work in print in classroom publications. It is always easier to write if one has an audience in mind, and the tedious tasks of editing and revising become not only bearable but essential when a writer knows that he is perfecting his work to facilitate the communication of his ideas to others.

An excellent form of publication that appeals particularly to children is the creation of their own, simply bound books. These may be produced as class projects or they may contain the work of individuals or small groups. They may be illustrated or decorated and include title pages, dedications, and tables of contents. Class anthologies of original stories, ballads, haiku, cinquain, and the like may be prepared throughout the year. A sympathetic librarian is likely to accept the books for circulation. Older children may create original stories and picture books for children in the primary grades. The stories of younger children may be printed out by the teacher on charts or sheets of oak tag for room displays. Stories and poems may be put on tape as a way to publish and preserve them for others' enjoyment. One class might share their stories and poems with another, presenting them in bound editions or staging prepared readings of them. A class newspaper or magazine is an excellent way to publish compositions of all kinds. Another form of publication is the "talking" newspaper or magazine, with the children recording on tape pieces they have written or otherwise composed.

Oral and Pictorial Composition
as Part of the Critical Process

Composition, whether in words, the movements of dance or mime, in paint or film, is essential exercise for the imagination. It may also be seen as an integral part of the process of literary criticism. Creative responses to literature—the acting out of key scenes in stories, miming to the rhythm of a poem, painting or drawing impressions of settings and characters, the creation of original dramas, paintings from the imagination, and mimes not directly related to a particular story or poem—are part of literary criticism. The groups of children who prepare a story for dramatization, for instance, are involved in a critical analysis of the structure of the story, deciding upon the key scenes to be dramatized and a coherent sequence for their presentation. Those who compose an original mime or drama must consider their story in terms of its beginning, middle, and end. How will the problem or conflict be introduced? How will it be resolved? How will the characters interrelate in the development of the plot? Thus, composition in other forms than words may embody a number of aspects central to the practice of elementary literary criticism, among them: enjoyment in experiencing, imaginative interpretation of individual works, creative composition, realization of form and structure in story.

The Use of Film in the
Elementary Literature Curriculum

All of the aspects of archetypal criticism that apply to printed stories, such as the concept of basic story "shapes" and the quest of the hero, apply as well to stories on film suitable for children as they do to stories in print. Children will be encouraged to draw upon their film experiences, in and out of school, during discussions of literary principles. Just as they can be taught to read printed stories perceptively, noting point of view, mood, tone, how characters are developed and how they interrelate, and the like, so they can be taught to "read" film with greater perception. The critical principle that stories must be first grasped as entities applies both to filmed and printed stories.

"Literature" on film and literature in print have a number of things in common, although each medium does make use of techniques that are unique to it. The film, with unusual juxtaposition of images, variations of length and angle of shots, and the like, can create a metaphorical language of association without using words. Films have a concentrated power of archetypal expression—the intensity of their symbolism is unmatched. Both types of creative expression employ images and symbols in similar ways: darkness and shadow symbolize the evil, menacing, or threatening; light and color are associated with their opposites. Landscapes and natural surroundings as well as weather are powerful images in creating mood and atmosphere. When the film-maker chooses to tell a story, his structural problems are similar to those of the author to the extent that he must find ways to begin, develop, and end his story. Since stories come in a limited number of basic shapes, the filmed story falls into one of the categories of comedy, romance, tragedy, or irony. The dialectical and cyclical structures of imagery are common to all types of literature. Thus, for variety, for enjoyment, and because the film is an important aspect of literature, particularly today, filmed literature should take its place with print in the elementary curriculum.

The composition of films by the children encompasses several aspects of the process of literary criticism. It involves a creative response as well as an analysis of the elements of story: character development, setting, tone, plot structure, point of view, and the like. If a printed story is to be adapted for filming, children must become aware of the story in terms of its structure; deciding, for instance, what scenes and characters are essential to the recreation of the story on film and which are not. When the project involves the creation of an original movie, the storytellers must consider how to structure their story: how and where it should begin, how and by whom the plot will be developed, how it should be ended. Usually, the first step in the creation of a film is the designing of a story board, a sequence of sketches that tell the story pictorially with instructions for the length and angle of each shot included in a caption. The story-board technique has obvious possibilities for teaching the children to trace a sequence of events and for helping them to see story in terms of structure and form. As a form of structural analysis this is exciting as well as profitable and it leads naturally into the shooting of films by the children themselves.

The use of filmed and printed literature together makes possible another form of literary criticism. Cross-media comparisons may be made between stories told in print and the films based on them.* The children will draw many conclusions about the unique charac-

*One example is *Evan's Corner* by Elizabeth Starr Hill.

teristics of each media. Films, for example, do not require descriptions of either the characters' appearance or the setting since the viewer sees these details for himself. In printed literature we are told what the character feels and thinks; film is more suited to showing us his physical reactions. Many children will find it interesting to discuss the relative merits of each medium. In a classroom where printed literature is a lively art, there will be none who see film as a substitute for it.

Chapter 9

A Postscript

Mathematics, music, physical education, social studies, science, and art all have their places in the elementary curriculum. They are firmly established as subjects of study, their content and methods of instruction receive serious consideration. It is not so with literature. Yet literature, of all man's creations, is one of the greatest sources of nourishment for developing minds and imaginations.

It has the capacity to delight; it is meant to be enjoyed, and children deserve every chance to revel in its pleasures. Literature is a humanistic study and studies in the humanities are essential to our survival in a technological world where things can easily become more important than people. Literature is a civilizing influence. Because it deals with human experience, because it has everything to do with people—their actions, their needs and desires—literature can show us both sides of the coin: what it means to be truly human and what it means to be inhumane. Because it is an art made of words, literature develops from and extends the aspect of man that separates him from all other animals, his language.

It is surely time to consider seriously the literary education of young children. It must be an education worthy of the name. It must be significant and systematic, with a sense of continuity; it cannot be piecemeal, but instead a piecing together of details that fit gradually into a meaningful design.

As we have seen, Northrop Frye's literary theory can be effectively put to use to make the earliest study of literature significant. Because it delineates the structural principles of literature, his scheme provides a means of unifying and integrating experience with literary works. It allows the student to look beyond this story or that poem to a vision of a whole that is greater than even the greatest of its parts. Surely the ability to see relationships and make connections is the essence of education in any field of study. Without a structure, experience is fragmentary and fleeting, a series of chance encounters that offer little in the way of genuine enlightenment.

It is important to emphasize again how inappropriate it would be to teach a complex literary theory directly to children. A knowledge of it enables *the teacher* to lead young critics to discover for themselves how literature works. It provides a method for approaching literary studies with purpose.

When literary criticism is treated seriously, we find that literature is placed firmly where it belongs: at the center of the elementary curriculum. The study of literature in all its aspects is the road to literacy. No detours are necessary. The child critic listens in wonder, reads with delight, responds to art with art. Of course, there can be no satisfactory results without commitment and a total commitment at that. Literature *is* the language art. All the other "language arts" are developed from and through it.

Unfortunately, it is radical today to insist that a program to develop literacy can and should be centered in literature, fiction and poetry in particular. Yet, children in large numbers have not thrived on instructional diets that serve up imaginative literature only as dessert. These children have turned to television to satisfy their desire for fantasy, their need to hear language that jingles, rhymes, and sings. For many of them reading is only an onerous exercise confined to classrooms.

Literature is the richest possible source of reading material. There is something for everyone among the thousands of children's books so readily available. There are stories and poems to echo every human feeling: desire for excitement and adventure, curiosity, fear, loneliness, jealousy, anger, hope, compassion, frustration, tenderness, rage. Feeling comes first.

Children want to read what makes them laugh or cry, shiver and gasp. They must have stories and poems that reflect what they themselves have felt. They need the thrill of imagining, of being for a time in some hero's shoes for a spine-tingling adventure. They deserve to experience the delight and amazement that comes with hearing language that puns and plays. For children reading must be equated with imagining, wondering, reacting feelingly. If it is not, we should not be surprised if they refuse to read.

A light touch must accompany all our efforts to teach literary criticism to children. Too heavy a hand, however scholarly, is as undesirable as it is unnecessary. Literature is an art and art is first of all to be experienced and savored. Even so, experience alone is not an adequate teacher. The study of literature takes place in the school and educators must concern themselves with growth and development. A knowledgeable adult who can guide this development is essential. As defined here, literary criticism is an all inclusive concept that includes experiencing literature, responding to it and creating it. Its practice does not depend upon commercially prepared programs or rigid timetables. No textbooks are necessary. What is needed to teach literary criticism is literature itself, genuine literature of all kinds and in great quantities. In this wealth of material all children will find some things that will compel them to listen, to read for themselves, to talk about what they have read, and to try to create literature of their own. An informed teacher is there to plan and structure presentations, to ask the right questions, to listen, to inspire, and to guide every creative effort.

The development of language ability, whether it be reading or writing, is a cumulative development. Unlike other studies, it develops from the inside out. When words engage our feelings and imaginations, we are motivated to read them. When our feelings and imaginings are stimulated, we have a need to use language to express them. That is why literature must play a major role in the development of our ability to make use of language. Words are powerful magic and nowhere is this magic more evident than in the language of literature. Literature, in partnership with the teacher who believes in its power, will work to produce those who are truly literate, readers and writers who are aware of the potential of language: its nature, its uses, its joy.

Bibliography

Selected Reference Books

Applebee, Arthur N. *The Child's Concept of Story: Ages Two to Seventeen.* Chicago: University of Chicago Press, 1978.

Well-documented studies of children's responses to literature.

Arbuthnot, May Hill, and others. *The Arbuthnot Anthology of Children's Literature,* 4th ed. Glenview, Ill.: Scott, Foresman, 1976.

An excellent selection of writing for children. Included in this volume is "Time for Poetry," one of the finest collections of poems for young people.

Arbuthnot, May Hill, and Sutherland, Zena. *Children and Books,* 5th ed. Glenview, Ill.: Scott, Foresman, 1977.

A basic source of information for teachers and parents. Includes discussion of all varieties of children's literature, criteria for evaluation and selection, methods of presentation, resources for further study.

Britton, James. *Prospect and Retrospect,* ed. by Gordon Pradl. London: Heinemann Educational Books, 1982.

Selected essays by the eminent scholar that deal with how we evolve maps of our worlds through language.

Chambers, Aidan. *Introducing Books to Children.* London: Heinemann Educational Books, 1973.

A practical look at ideas, methods, and approaches that bring books and young people into contact.

Chukovsky, Kornei. *From Two to Five*, trans. by Miriam Morton. Berkeley: University of California Press, 1963.

> A Russian poet's sensitive discussion of young children's language and thought. Emphasizes the importance of imaginative literature in a child's development.

Frye, Northrop. *Anatomy of Criticism: Four Essays.* Princeton: Princeton University Press, 1957.

> This revolutionary book gives "a synoptic view of the scope, theory, principles, and techniques of literary criticism." An attempt to establish order in a disorderly field, it sets forth principles to inform the teaching of literature.

Frye, Northrop. *The Educated Imagination.* Bloomington: Indiana University Press, 1964.

> The distinguished literary critic discusses, in six lectures originally broadcast by the Canadian Broadcasting Corporation, the central role played by literature in the development of the imagination. In one of the lectures, Frye presents his views on the order and content appropriate in literary studies for children.

Frye, Northrop. *The Great Code: The Bible and Literature.* New York: Harcourt Brace Jovanovich, 1982.

> A study of the Bible as the single most important influence in the imaginative tradition of Western literature.

Frye, Northrop, supervisory ed. *Literature: Uses of the Imagination.* New York: Harcourt Brace Jovanovich, 1973.

> Eleven pupil anthologies with accompanying teacher's manuals provide a sequential program for the study of literature in grades seven through twelve. An innovative program based upon the literary theory of Northrop Frye.

Frye, Northrop. *Spiritus Mundi.* Bloomington and London: Indiana University Press, 1976.

> A dozen major essays about literature and its context.

Frye, Northrop. *The Stubborn Structure: Essays on Criticism and Society.* Ithaca: Cornell University Press, 1970.

> A collection of essays and lectures dealing with the contexts of literary criticism and specific studies in literature. Of particu-

lar interest to teachers is an essay on the teaching of literature, "Elementary Teaching and Elemental Scholarship."

Frye, Northrop. *The Well-Tempered Critic.* Bloomington: Indiana University Press, 1963.

Three essays dealing with styles of language and the teaching of literature. Emphasizes the importance of poetry as the basis of a literary education.

Graves, Donald. *Writing: Teachers and Children at Work.* London and Exeter, N.H.: Heinemann Educational Books, 1982.

Based on extended classroom studies of how children write, with insights into what adults can do to help them.

Hardy, Barbara. *Storytellers and Listeners.* New York: Athlone Press, 1975.

Hardy argues that narrative is a primary act of mind transferred *to* art *from* life.

Hazard, Paul. *Books, Children and Men,* 4th ed. Boston: Horn Book, 1960.

A classic plea for children's right to read for pleasure books of their own choice.

Holbrook, David. *English for Maturity,* 2nd ed. New York: Cambridge University Press, 1967.

A British educator's plea for fresh and vital approaches to the teaching of English. Although the book discusses teaching in secondary schools, its sound pedagogy is applicable and adaptable to elementary classrooms.

Holdaway, Don. *The Foundations of Literacy.* Sydney, Australia: Ashton Scholastic, 1979.

A fresh perspective on many of the complex and disputed issues related to the development of literacy.

Johnson, Edna; Sickels, Evelyn R.; and Sayers, Frances Clarke. *Anthology of Children's Literature,* 5th ed. Boston: Houghton Mifflin, 1977.

A distinguished collection of the poetry and prose written for children. The brief, well-written scholarly introductions to each section are an outstanding feature of this fine anthology.

Koch, Kenneth. *Rose, Where Did You Get That Red?* New York: Vintage Books, 1973.

> A poet describes his enlightened methods of teaching great poetry to children. Includes examples of the original poetry students wrote in response to inspired teaching of fine literature.

Koch, Kenneth. *Wishes, Lies and Dreams.* New York: Chelsea House, 1970.

> Using numerous examples of children's work, the poet tells how he went into city classrooms to "free children to write poetry."

Langer, Susanne K. *Philosophy in a New Key.* New York: New American Library, 1948.

> This book includes a stimulating discussion of discursive and non-discursive language. In the chapter "Language," the author gives support to the thesis that the expressive use of language precedes the utilitarian.

Moffett, James. *Teaching the Universe of Discourse.* Boston: Houghton Mifflin, 1968; reprint, 1983.

> Discussion of how language, a symbol system not a content subject, is learned through manipulation rather than analysis.

Moffett, James, and Wagner, Betty Jane. *Student-Centered Language Arts and Reading, K–13: A Handbook for Teachers,* 3rd ed. Boston: Houghton Mifflin, 1976.

> A comprehensive text on the teaching of all aspects of language.

Odland, Norine. *Teaching Literature in the Elementary School.* Urbana, Ill.: National Council of Teachers of English, 1969.

> The author reviews relevant research, curriculum trends, teaching materials, the judgments of recognized experts in the field, reports and findings from various national committees and commissions in an attempt to answer the question "Where are we?" The answer, unfortunately, is: We have a long way to go before we can say we teach literature in the elementary school.

Opie, Iona and Peter. *The Lore and Language of School Children.* New York: Oxford University Press, 1959.

> A fascinating record of the school child's strange and primitive culture including innumerable rhymes and chants, catcalls, stock jokes, riddles, and slang epithets. Comprehensive, scholarly, and exceedingly readable.

Pitcher, Evelyn Goodenough, and Prelinger, Ernst. *Children Tell Stories: An Analysis of Fantasy.* New York: International Universities Press, 1963.

> This collection of stories, written by boys and girls from two to five, brings to light the subjective experience of little children.

Vandergrift, K. E. *Child and Story: The Literary Connection.* New York: Neal-Schuman, 1980.

> The importance of story in a child's life, story as a literary form, and the practice of criticism are the major themes of this comprehensive, well-researched book.

Wilkinson, Andrew. *The Foundations of Language.* London: Oxford University Press, 1971.

> Language and its educational implications, particularly its relationship to reading and the problems of learning to read.

Wolsch, Robert. *Poetic Composition Through the Grades.* New York: Teachers College Press, 1970.

> A program to develop poetic composition that is built upon the conviction that poetry is an essential ingredient in the development of literacy and the imagination.

Children's Books and Stories

Adopted Jane by Helen Fern Daringer (Harcourt Brace Jovanovich, 1947).

The Adventures of Huckleberry Finn by Mark Twain (Harper, 1931).

Alice's Adventures in Wonderland by Lewis Carroll with illus. by John Tenniel (Macmillan, 1966).

And Now Miguel by Joseph Krumgold with illus. by Jean Charlot (Thomas Y. Crowell, 1953).

"Balder, The Death of" in *Thunder of the Gods* by Dorothy Hosford with illus. by Claire and George Loudon (Holt, Rinehart & Winston, 1952).

The Bears' House by Marilyn Sachs with illus. by Louis Glanzman (Doubleday, 1971).

"Beauty and the Beast" in *The Blue Fairy Book* by Andrew Lang with illus. by Ben Kutcher (Longman, 1948).

Beowulf by Rosemary Sutcliff with illus. by Charles Keeping (Dutton, 1962).

Blue Willow by Doris Gates with illus. by Paul Lantz (Viking Press, 1940).

"Boots and His Brothers" in *Popular Tales from the Norse* by P. C. Asbjörnson and trans. by G. W. Dasent (Putnam, 1908).

Boris by Jap Ter Haar, trans. by Martha Mearns with illus. by Rien Poorvliet (Delacorte, 1970).

The Borrowers by Mary Norton with illus. by Beth and Joe Krush (Harcourt Brace Jovanovich, 1953).

The Bronze Bow by Elizabeth Speare (Houghton Mifflin, 1961).

Call It Courage by Armstrong Sperry with illus. by the author (Macmillan, 1940).

The Carrot Seed by Ruth Krauss with illus. by Crockett Johnson (Harper, 1945).

Charlie and the Chocolate Factory by Roald Dahl with illus. by Joseph Schindelman (Alfred A. Knopf, 1964).

Charlotte's Web by E. B. White with illus. by Garth Williams (Harper, 1952).

A Christmas Carol by Charles Dickens with illus. by Arthur Rackam (Lippincott, 1952).

Cinderella trans. from Charles Perrault with illus. by Marcia Brown (Scribner's, 1954).

Come to the Edge by Julia Cunningham (Pantheon, 1977).

The Courage of Sarah Noble by Alice Dalgleish with illus. by Leonard Weisgard (Scribner's, 1954).

The Dark is Rising by Susan Cooper with illus. by Alan E. Cober (Atheneum, 1973).

David and Goliath retold by Beatrice Schenk de Regniers with illus. by Richard M. Powers (Viking Press, 1965).

Dick Whittington and His Cat written and cut in linoleum by Marcia Brown (Scribner's, 1950).

Dinky Hocker Shoots Smack by M. E. Kerr (Harper & Row, 1972).

Dominic by William Steig with illus. by the author (Farrar, Straus & Giroux, 1972).

Dorp Dead by Julia Cunningham with illus. by James Spanfeller (Pantheon, 1965).

The Dragon Takes a Wife by Walter Dean Myers with illus. by Ann Grifalconi (Bobbs-Merrill, 1972).

"Drakestail" in *The Red Fairy Book* by Andrew Lang with illus. by Marc Simont (Longman, 1948).

Drummer Hoff adapted by Barbara Emberley with illus. by Ed Emberley (Prentice-Hall, 1967).

Edgar Allen by John Neufeld (S. G. Phillips, 1968).

Ellen Grae by Vera and Bill Cleaver with illus. by Ellen Raskin (Lippincott, 1967).

The Emperor's New Clothes by Hans Christian Andersen with illus. by Virginia Lee Burton (Houghton Mifflin, 1949).

A Figure of Speech by Norma Fox Mazer (Delacorte, 1973).

The 500 Hats of Bartholomew Cubbins by Dr. Seuss with illus. by the author (Random House, 1938).

"The Flea" in *Picture Tales from Spain* by Ruth Sawyer (Lippincott, 1936).

The Flight of the Doves by Walter Macken (Macmillan, 1968).

Freaky Friday by Mary Rodgers (Harper & Row, 1972).

(George) by E. L. Konigsburg with illus. by the author (Atheneum, 1970).

Gilgamesh: Man's First Story by Bernarda Bryson with illus. by the author (Holt, Rinehart & Winston, 1967).

The Gingerbread Boy illus. by William Curtis Holdsworth (Farrar, Straus & Giroux, 1968).

The Goose Girl from the Brothers Grimm with illus. by Marguerite de Angeli (Doubleday, 1964).

Gulliver's Travels by Jonathan Swift (Grossett & Dunlop).

Hansel and Gretel from the Brothers Grimm with illus. by William Chappell (Alfred A. Knopf, 1944).

Harriet Tubman: Conductor on the Underground Railway by Ann Petry (Thomas Y. Crowell, 1955).

"Henny Penny" in *English Fairy Tales* by Joseph Jacobs with illus. by John Batten (Putnam, 1898).

Henry 3 by Joseph Krumgold with illus. by Alvin Smith (Atheneum, 1967).

"Hercules" in *The Twelve Labors of Hercules* told by Robert Newman with illus. by Charles Keeping (Thomas Y. Crowell, 1972).

How Many Miles to Babylon by Paula Fox with illus. by Paul Giovanopoulos (David White, 1967).

The Hundred Dresses by Eleanor Estes with illus. by Louis Slobodkin (Harcourt Brace Jovanovich, 1944).

The Iliad of Homer retold by Barbara Leonie Picard with illus. by Joan Kiddell-Monroe (Henry Z. Walck, 1960).

Inside My Feet: The Story of a Giant by Richard Kennedy with illus. by Ronald Himler (Harper & Row, 1979).

It's Like This, Cat by Emily Neville with illus. by Emily Weiss (Harper & Row, 1963).

Jason, Clashing Rocks: The Story of, by Ian Serraillier with illus. by William Stobbs (Henry Z. Walck, 1964).

The Jazz Man by Mary Weik with illus. by Ann Grifalconi (Atheneum, 1966).

John Henry, An American Legend by Ezra Jack Keats with illus. by the author (Pantheon, 1965).

Journey Outside by Mary Q. Steele with woodcuts by Rocco Negri (Viking Press, 1969).

The Judge by Harve Zemach with illus. by Margot Zemach (Farrar, Straus & Giroux, 1969).

Julie of the Wolves by Jean Craighead George with illus. by John Schoenherr (Harper & Row, 1972).

Just So Stories by Rudyard Kipling with illus. by Joseph M. Gleeson (Doubleday, 1912).

King Arthur and His Knights, The Story of, by Howard Pyle with illus. by the author (Scribner's, 1903).

Konrad by Christine Nostlinger, trans. by Anthea Bell with illus. by Carol Nicklaus (Watts, 1977).

Leo, the Late Bloomer by Robert Kraus with illus. by Jose Aruego (Windmill Books/Abelard-Schuman, 1971).

Little Bear by Else Holmelund Minarik with illus. by Maurice Sendak (Harper, 1957).

Little House in the Big Woods and *Little House on the Prairie* by Laura Ingalls Wilder with illus. by Garth Williams (Harper, 1953).

Little Red Riding Hood from the Brothers Grimm retold and illus. by Harriet Pincus (Harcourt Brace Jovanovich, 1968).

Little Tim and the Brave Sea Captain by Edward Ardizzone with illus. by the author (Henry Z. Walck, 1955).

Little Toot by Hardie Gramatky with illus. by the author (Putnam, 1939).

The Loner by Ester Wier with illus. by Christine Price (David McKay, 1963).

Mary Jane by Dorothy Sterling with illus. by Ernest Crichlow (Doubleday, 1959).

Millions of Cats by Wanda Gág with illus. by the author (Coward, McCann, 1928).

"Molly Whuppie" in *English Fairy Tales* by Joseph Jacobs (Putnam, 1892).

Mom, the Wolfman and Me by Norma Klein (Pantheon, 1972).

Moses by Katherine Shippen (Harper, 1949).

Nobody's Family's Going To Change by Louise Fitzhugh (Farrar, 1974).

North to Freedom by Anne Holm and trans. by L. W. Kingsland (Harcourt Brace Jovanovich, 1965).

Odysseus the Wanderer retold by Aubrey de Sélincourt (Criterion, 1965).

"Old Man and the Beginning of the World" in *Indian Legends from the Northern Rockies* by Ella E. Clark (University of Oklahoma Press, 1966).

Padre Porko by Robert Davis (Holiday House, 1948).

Paul Bunyan in *Ol' Paul: The Mighty Logger* by Glen Rounds with illus. by the author (Holiday House, 1949).

Pecos Bill and Lightning compiled by Leigh Peck with illus. by Kurt Wiese (Houghton Mifflin, 1940).

"Perseus" in *The Heroes* by Charles Kingsley with illus. by Joan Kiddell-Monroe (Dutton, 1963).

Peter Rabbit, The Tale of, by Beatrix Potter with illus. by the author (Frederick Warne, 1902).

Pigeon, Fly Home by Thomas Liggett (Holiday House, 1956).

The Pigman by Paul Zindel (Harper & Row, 1968).

"Prometheus the Firebringer" in *Orpheus with His Lute* by W. M. L. Hutchinson (Longman, 1926).

The Pushcart War by Jean Merrill with illus. by Ronni Solbert (Young Scott, 1964).

Puss in Boots trans. from Charles Perrault with illus. by Marcia Brown (Scribner's, 1952).

Queenie Peavy by Robert Burch with illus. by Jerry Lazare (Viking Press, 1966).

Rapunzel from the Brothers Grimm with illus. by Felix Hoffmann (Harcourt Brace Jovanovich, 1961).

Roland, The Horn of, by Jay Williams with illus. by Sean Morrison (Thomas Y. Crowell, 1968).

Rufus M. by Eleanor Estes with illus. by Louis Slobodkin (Harcourt Brace Jovanovich, 1941).

St. George and the Dragon by Edmund Spenser, retold by Sandol Stoddard Warburg with illus. by Pauline Baynes (Houghton Mifflin, 1963).

Shadow of a Bull by Maia Wojciechowska with illus. by Alvin Smith (Atheneum, 1964).

The Shrinking of Treehorn by Florence Perry Heide with illus. by Edward Gorey (Holiday House, 1971).

Siegfried, The Treasure of, by E. M. Almedingen with illus. by Charles Keeping (Lippincott, 1965).

"Sigurd" in *Sons of the Volsungs* adapted by Dorothy Hosford from *Sigurd the Volsung* by William Morris with illus. by Frank Dobias (Holt, Rinehart & Winston, 1949).

The Sleeping Beauty from the Brothers Grimm with illus. by Felix Hoffmann (Harcourt Brace Jovanovich, 1960).

Snow White and the Seven Dwarfs from the Brothers Grimm, trans. by Randall Jarrell with illus. by Nancy Ekholm Berkert (Farrar, Straus & Giroux, 1972).

"Soldier Jack" from *Jack Tales* by Richard Chase (Houghton Mifflin, 1943).

Sounder by William H. Armstrong with illus. by James Barkley (Harper & Row, 1969).

"Steadfast Tin Soldier" in *Hans Andersen's Fairy Tales* trans. by L. W. Kingsland with illus. by Ernest H. Shepard (Henry Z. Walck, 1962).

The Stonecutter by Gerald McDermott with illus. by the author (Viking, 1975).

Stone Fox by John Reynolds Gardiner with illus. by Marcia Sewall (Crowell, 1980).

The Summer Birds by Penelope Farmer (Harcourt, 1962).

Theseus, The Way of Danger: The Story of, by Ian Serraillier with illus. by William Stobbs (Henry Z. Walck, 1963).

The Three Bears, The Story of, with illus. by Leslie Brooke (Frederick Warne, 1905).

The Three Billy Goats Gruff by P. C. Asbjörnsen and J. E. Moe with illus. by Marcia Brown (Harcourt Brace Jovanovich, 1957).

The Three Little Pigs with illus. by William Pene du Bois (Viking Press, 1962).

Too Much Noise by Ann McGovern with illus. by Simms Taback (Houghton Mifflin, 1967).

The Trumpet of the Swan by E. B. White with illus. by Edward Frascino (Harper & Row, 1970).

Tuck Everlasting by Natalie Babbitt (Farrar, 1975).

Tuned Out by Maia Wojciechowska (Harper & Row, 1968).

The Ugly Duckling by Hans Christian Andersen, trans. by R. P. Keigwin with illus. by Johannes Larsen (Macmillan, 1967).

Where the Wild Things Are by Maurice Sendak with illus. by the author (Harper & Row, 1963).

Wild in the World by John Donovan (Harper & Row, 1972).

A Wrinkle in Time by Madeleine L'Engle (Farrar, 1962).

Index

165